5TH AND 6TH GRADE

Spring 1994

Teachers Guide

STRUGGLES KIDS FACE

NEW LIFE IN CHRIST

SUCCESS AND FAILURE

Loveland, Colorado

Hands-On Bible Curriculum™, Spring 1994
Copyright © 1994 Group Publishing, Inc.

First Printing

Credits
Edited by Mike Nappa
Cover designed by Liz Howe and DeWain Stoll
Designed by Dori Walker and Lisa Smith
Cartoons by Daryll Collins
Illustrations by Amy Bryant and Elizabeth Woodworth
Posters by Bron Smith, Amy Bryant, and Lisa Smith
Copyedited by Stephanie G'Schwind
Typeset by Pat Reinheimer

Scripture quoted from The Youth Bible, New Century Version, copyright © 1991 by Word Publishing, Dallas, Texas 75039. Used by permission.

ISBN 1-55945-346-X
Printed in the United States of America

CONTENTS

HOW TO USE THIS BOOK

WHY HANDS-ON BIBLE CURRICULUM™?

There's nothing more exciting than helping kids develop a relationship with Jesus Christ. But keeping fifth- and sixth-graders interested in Bible study and Christian growth can be a challenge. Many kids drop out at this age, complaining that Bible lessons are boring—just more of the same old thing. Teachers tell us they're desperate for something that works.

We've found a way to get kids excited about studying the Bible. Each quarter of Hands-On Bible Curriculum is packed with fresh, creative, *active* programming that will capture kids' interest and keep them coming back for more.

Here's why Hands-On Bible Curriculum will work for you.

A NEW APPROACH TO LEARNING

Research shows that kids remember about 90 percent of what they *do* but less than 10 percent of what they *hear*. What does this say to us? Simply that kids don't learn by being lectured at! They need to be actively involved in lively experiences that bring home the lesson's point.

Group's Hands-On Bible Curriculum uses a unique approach to Christian education called active learning. In each session, students participate in a variety of fun and memorable learning experiences that help them understand one important point. As each activity unfolds, kids discover and internalize biblical truths. Because they're *doing* instead of just listening, kids remember what they learn.

Your students will be fascinated with the neat gadgets and gizmos packed in the Learning Lab®. And you'll feel good about seeing kids grow spiritually while they're having fun. To build excitement, keep the contents of the Learning Lab under cover. Kids will keep wondering what strange and wonderful gizmos you'll pull out for next week's lesson.

All the activities are designed to work with classes of any size, although we recommend having at least one teacher for every 12 students. The items in the Learning Lab may be used in several lessons, so be sure to hang on to them until this teachers guide informs you they won't be needed in future lessons.

In each lesson, you'll find a photocopiable "Table Tent™" to send home with kids. Besides providing an important link between home and church, the "Table Tent" has great cartoons, "Talk Triggers," and daily Scripture readings to get kids and parents talking about The Point of the lesson. You can encourage parents' involvement during the next 13 weeks by mailing photocopies of the letter to parents found on page 10.

The items listed below are typical supplies that may be used in the lessons in this book. All other items required for teaching are included in the Learning Lab. We recommend your students use their own Bibles in this course so they can discover for themselves the value and relevance of the Scriptures.

- ◆ Bible reference materials (such as Bible concordances or dictionaries)
- ◆ candles
- ◆ cassette player
- ◆ cellophane tape
- ◆ chalkboard and chalk
- ◆ masking tape
- ◆ glue or glue stick
- ◆ markers
- ◆ matches
- ◆ newsprint
- ◆ old magazines
- ◆ old newspapers
- ◆ paper clips
- ◆ pencils
- ◆ paper cups
- ◆ plain paper
- ◆ scissors
- ◆ snacks
- ◆ stapler
- ◆ 3×5 cards
- ◆ trash cans

SUCCESSFUL TEACHING: YOU CAN DO IT!

What does active learning mean to you as a teacher? It takes a lot of pressure off because the spotlight shifts from you to the students. Instead of being the principal player, you become a guide and facilitator—a choreographer of sorts! These ideas will get you started in your new role:

◆ **Be creative in your use of classroom space.** Move tables aside so kids can move around freely and work in groups.

◆ **Think about open areas in the church** that might be available for activities—the foyer, the front of the sanctuary, a side yard, or a parking lot. Kids love variety; a different setting can bring new life and excitement to your lessons.

◆ **Be sure to help kids tie each experience to The Point of each lesson.** The printed discussion questions and summary statements will help students explore their feelings, discover important principles, and decide how to apply these principles to their lives.

◆ **Don't forget to say The Point.** It's important to say The Point just as it's written in each activity. Repeating The Point over and over throughout the lesson will help kids remember it and apply it to their lives.

◆ **Remember that kids learn in different ways.** So don't shy away from an activity just because you've never done anything like it before. It may be just what's needed to help one of your students get The Point.

◆ **Use active listening to help kids process the activities.** Follow up kids' responses to discussion questions by asking, "What did you mean by that?" and "Can you tell me more?"

◆ **Get to know your students.** When you meet your class members for the first time, get to know them by name. Ask a fun question such as "If you were an animal, what would you be and why?" to help kids get to know each other better.

And when new students show up from week to week, welcome them to the class and help them feel at home. Your sincere interest in each class member will greatly enhance the experiences you'll share in the next 13 weeks.

◆ **Call kids by name.** Make an effort to personalize learning by calling kids by their names during the lessons. If you have trouble remembering names or have new kids each week, consider using name tags.

◆ **Know your kids' abilities and needs.** The chart on page 9 will help you know a bit more about the needs, wants, and abilities of your students.

◆ **Make your class a "safe zone" for kids with special needs and learning disabilities.** Avoid calling on students to read or pray aloud if they find it embarrassing.

◆ **Capitalize on your students' strengths.** A student who doesn't read well may be a terrific song leader for your class. A shy, introverted student may have wonderful insights and the ability to resolve difficult issues. Learn to let your students shine by drawing on their strengths and allowing each of them to make positive contributions to the class.

◆ **If kids seem reluctant to talk** during discussion times, try offering a controversial answer to spark more responses. Or, have your students take 30 seconds of "think time." Then call on someone by name to begin the discussion.

◆ **If your kids can't seem to stop talking,** tell them they have 30 seconds to say one last thing about the subject at hand. Or, use the signal for that lesson, then tell kids it's time to wrap up the discussion and move on.

◆ **Be aware of the attitudes kids bring into class.** Some kids may walk in after a family fight or a disappointing experience at school. Encourage kids to share their feelings. Then be patient as they work to overcome their bad day.

ATTENTION, PLEASE!

Stand back and get ready for a radical idea: Noise can be a good thing in Sunday school! Educators will tell you that kids process new information best by interacting with each other. Having kids quiet and still doesn't necessarily mean your class is a success. A better clue might be seeing happy, involved, excited students moving around the classroom, discussing how to apply to their lives the new truths they're learning. But if noise and activity are good, how does a teacher keep control?

Good question! And we've got some good answers.

◆ **Keep things moving!** Most kids have about a seven-minute attention span—the amount of time between TV commercials. That means you need to be ready to move on to the next activity *before* kids get bored with the current one.

◆ **Don't show kids the contents of the Learning Lab too soon.** Keep curiosity at a peak by bringing Learning Lab items out of the box one by one as needed for the lesson.

◆ **Establish attention-getting signals.** Flashing the lights or raising your hand will let kids know it's time to stop what they're doing and look at you. You'll find a suggestion for a signal in the introduction to the first four-week module. You can use this signal throughout all 13 weeks. Rehearse the signal with your students at the beginning of each class. Once your kids become familiar with the signal, regaining their attention will become an automatic classroom ritual.

◆ **Participate—don't just observe.** Your enthusiasm will draw kids into an activity and help them see you as a friend, not just someone in authority.

◆ **Look for teachable moments.** An activity that seems to be a flop may provide a wonderful opportunity for learning if you ask questions such as "Why didn't this work out?" "How is this like what happens in real life?" or "What can we learn from this experience?"

◆ **Make the lessons work for your class.** Use the Bonus Ideas found on page 161 or the Time Stuffers found in the module introductions to lengthen a lesson. The lessons can also be shortened if you have a large class or a short class session. Simply pick the activities that'll work best with your kids and leave the other activities out. If you find time running short during a lesson, move on to the closing. Since you make The Point during each activity, you'll have taught something significant even if you don't get through the whole lesson.

◆ **Adapt the lessons to your class size.** While each activity works with larger classes, the bigger the class size, the more time the activity will take. Save time by not having every student respond to every question.

◆ **Use the Time Stuffers.** These independent-learning activities will keep kids occupied (and learning!)
- ✔ when they arrive early,
- ✔ when an individual or a group finishes an activity before the others, or
- ✔ when there is extra time after the lesson.

You'll find a Time Stuffer in the introduction to each module. After a quick setup, kids can use the activity during all the lessons of the four- or five-week module.

◆ **Rely on the Holy Spirit to help you.** Don't be afraid of kids' questions. Remember the best answers are those the kids find themselves—not the ones teachers spoon-feed them.

UNDERSTANDING YOUR FIFTH- AND SIXTH-GRADERS

MENTAL DEVELOPMENT

◆ Well-developed critical-thinking and problem-solving skills.
◆ Beginning to question authority figures; prefer to reason things through for themselves.
◆ Interested in how past and present world events affect their lives.

SOCIAL DEVELOPMENT

◆ Spend a lot of time with one best friend.
◆ Usually prefer to stick to same-sex friendships.
◆ Thrive on organized games and group activities.

EMOTIONAL DEVELOPMENT

◆ Frequently get mixed messages about being a child or being mature and ready to accept responsibility for choices and actions.
◆ Subject to strong fears about losing a parent, being abandoned, being rejected by friends, being a victim of violence, or becoming ill.
◆ Strongly influenced by heroes and role models.

PHYSICAL DEVELOPMENT

◆ High energy levels demand a lot of physical activity.
◆ Girls tend to be taller and more physically developed; boys often find this intimidating and tend to avoid physical contact with girls.

SPIRITUAL DEVELOPMENT

◆ Want everything to be fair.
◆ Want to test what they've been taught about God against their own experiences.
◆ Able to make choices about finding God's will and following it.

Dear Parent,

I'm so glad to be your child's teacher this quarter. With our Hands-On Bible Curriculum, your child will look at Bible study in a whole new way.

For the next 13 weeks we'll explore what Scripture has to say to fifth- and sixth-graders about struggles kids face, new life in Christ, and success and failure. Using active-learning methods and a surprising assortment of gadgets and gizmos (such as a twirlybird, flippers, and a carpenter wreath), we'll help kids discover meaningful applications of God's Word.

Our Hands-On Bible Curriculum welcomes you to play an important part in what your child learns. **Each week kids will receive a "Table Tent" to take home and share.** The "Table Tent" is a single sheet of paper containing brief Bible readings for each day of the week, thought-provoking "Talk Triggers," and a cartoon—all focused on The Point of our Bible lesson for the week.

Let me encourage you to fold the "Table Tent" on the fold lines and set it in a prominent place. Use it regularly; it's a great tool for reinforcing Bible truths and promoting positive, healthy communication in your family.

Sincerely,

**TABLE™
TENT**

STRUGGLES KIDS FACE

BY
SUSAN GROVER

Wouldn't it be great if you could arrange for your kids to grow up in Disneyland? Lots of friendly people, exciting entertainment, and any kind of fast-food you could imagine. They'd be safe and protected from all of life's struggles. But that's not the way God planned it. Each of your students will face difficult problems, worries, and fearful situations.

Fifth- and sixth-graders today deal with tougher, more serious issues than kids did 20 years ago. According to a Search Institute survey of fifth- and sixth-graders, 41 to 52 percent of kids worry about hunger and poverty. Forty-eight to 50 percent worry that a parent might die. And 37 to 43 percent worry about violence.

You may not be able to shelter your kids in Disneyland, but you can do something far better. You can teach them that in times of need, Jesus is an ever-present help. Use these four lessons to show your group members how to rely on God in the midst of life's struggles.

━ FOUR LESSONS ON STRUGGLES KIDS FACE ━

LESSON	PAGE	THE POINT	THE BIBLE BASIS
1—Beating the Bully Factor	13	God can help us face people who intimidate us.	Psalm 124
2—Never-Ending Blues?	23	God cares when we're feeling down.	Psalm 34:17-19
3—Dealing With Family Crises	33	God can heal hurting families.	Psalm 23
4—What Did You Say?	45	What we say reflects who we are.	Psalm 34:11-14

LEARNING LAB

THE SIGNAL

During the lessons on Struggles Kids Face, your signal to get kids' attention will be to squeeze the *squeaker* found in the Learning Lab. In response to the *squeaker,* have kids immediately stop what they're doing, raise their hands, and focus on you.

Tell kids about this signal—and practice it—before the lesson begins. Explain that it's important to respond to this signal quickly so the class can do as many fun activities as possible. During the lessons, you'll be prompted when to use the signal.

LEARNING LAB

THE TIME STUFFER

This module's Time Stuffer will encourage kids to look for the weapons of their faith when they encounter struggles. Hang the *Struggle Busters!* poster (found in the Learning Lab) in a prominent place in the room. During their free moments, kids can search the poster to find the symbols that represent the weapons of faith listed in **Ephesians 6:10-18.**

BEATING THE BULLY FACTOR

THE POINT

God can help us face people who intimidate us.

THE BIBLE BASIS

Psalm 124

> What if the Lord had not been on our side? (Let Israel repeat this.) What if the Lord had not been on our side when we were attacked? When they were angry with us, they would have swallowed us alive. They would have been like a flood drowning us; they would have poured over us like a river. They would have swept us away like a mighty stream. Praise the Lord, who did not let them chew us up. We escaped like a bird from the hunter's trap. The trap broke, and we escaped. Our help comes from the Lord, who made heaven and earth.

In **Psalm 124,** King David reflects on his past military victories. "What if the Lord had not been on our side?" he muses. The result would have been disaster. But God *didn't* abandon David. In the face of powerful enemies, God intervened and helped David overcome those who sought to harm him. No wonder David could confidently proclaim, "Our help comes from the Lord."

For fifth- and sixth-graders, enemies come in the form of bullies—not foreign armies. For James, the bully is an older student who delights in pushing and shoving. For Lisa, the bully is a group of kids who torment her with teasing and put-downs. For Kerry, the bully is a teacher who ridicules her attempts at creative expression.

Students need to understand they're not alone in fearful and intimidating situations such as these. Use this lesson to show kids how they, like David, can confidently proclaim, "Our help comes from the Lord."

Other Scriptures used in the lesson are **Matthew 5:43-48; 1 Thessalonians 5:15-16;** and **Psalm 3:3-6.**

GETTING THE POINT

Students will
◆ discuss what they'd do in intimidating situations,
◆ examine a biblical response to enemies, and
◆ brainstorm tactics for dealing with bullies.

THIS LESSON AT A GLANCE

SECTION	MINUTES	WHAT STUDENTS WILL DO	LEARNING LAB SUPPLIES	CLASSROOM SUPPLIES
ATTENTION GRABBER	5 to 10	**Designated Bullies**—Play a game where some students are "picked on" and some aren't.	Elastic strips, flippers, squeaker	Masking tape
BIBLE EXPLORATION AND APPLICATION	8 to 13	**Bully Buster**—Examine Psalm 124 after deciding what to do in intimidating situations.	Cassette: "Bully Buster"	Bibles, cassette player, newsprint, marker
	10 to 15	**Blow Me Down!**—Gang up on each other during a game and discuss Matthew 5:43-48 and 1 Thessalonians 5:15-16.	Flippers	Bibles, masking tape, paper, pencils
	7 to 12	**Bully Shield**—Decide on tactics to "shield" each other from bullies and discuss how God is described as a shield in Psalm 3:3-6.		Bibles, paper, pencils
CLOSING	5 to 10	**Three Cheers for Us**—Cheer for each other to be encouraging friends.	Mini straw hat	

Remember to make photocopies of the "Table Tent" handout (p. 22) to send home with your kids. The "Table Tent" is a valuable tool for helping fifth- and sixth-graders talk with their parents about what they're learning in class.

THE LESSON

Before the lesson, collect the necessary items from the Learning Lab for the activities you plan to use. Refer to the pictures in the margins to see what each item looks like.

ATTENTION GRABBER

DESIGNATED BULLIES

(5 to 10 minutes)

Begin class by teaching students the signal for this quarter. Tell kids that whenever you sound the *squeaker,* they're to stop what they're doing, raise their hands, and focus on you. Practice the signal two or three times.

Then say: **We're going to start today with a game to get us thinking about our topic.**

Form two teams (a team should be at least two people) and mark a starting line on the floor with masking tape. Have teams stand single file behind the line. Give the first person in each line a *flipper.* Put a chair about 10 feet in front of each team.

Next, select a volunteer from each team to act as a "designated bully" during the game. Give each bully an *elastic strip* and tell everyone that the volunteers can choose one or two opposing team members to "pick on" during the game. A designated bully "picks on" others by using the *elastic strips* to either blindfold opposing team members or tie their hands together as they're about to begin their turns.

Say: **The object of this game is for each teammate to flip the *flipper* on the floor, around the chair, and back to the next person in line. The first team to have all its members successfully complete the task is the winner. Encourage your teammates by cheering them on. Stop when you hear the *squeaker.* Ready? Go.**

When the game is over, applaud the winners and collect the Learning Lab items for later use. Gather everyone and ask:

◆ **What did you think of this game?** (It was fun; I was bummed because I got picked on; I was worried the bullies might pick on me.)

◆ **What did you do to help your team overcome being picked on?** (I cheered louder for the ones who were picked on; I went as fast as I could on my turn; I tried to shout directions to my teammates who got picked on.)

LEARNING LAB

TEACHER TIP

If you feel it's necessary, remind the designated bullies not to get too rough during this activity. Make sure the "picked on" students cooperate with the bullies as well.

Also, it's best to have kids play the game on their hands and knees. If your class is made up of more than 12 students, you might want to form four teams for this activity. Refer to the diagram in the margin to help you teach kids how to flip the *flippers.*

◆ **How does this game compare to your experiences with real bullies?** (This was no big deal because we knew the bullies couldn't really hurt us; we can help each other overcome bullies.)

Say: **Everyone must deal with bullies of one kind or another. Some bullies intimidate us, or make us afraid, with the threat of violence. Others like to pick on us with words or pranks. Today we're going to learn more about how God can help us face people who intimidate us.**

I've got lots of fun and interesting things planned, so be sure to help each other respond quickly to the signal during class. That way we'll be able to do everything and get the most out of today's lesson.

THE **POINT** ✍

BIBLE EXPLORATION AND APPLICATION

LEARNING LAB

BULLY BUSTER

(8 to 13 minutes)

Form pairs and have partners sit together on the floor. Say: **I'm going to play three segments from the *cassette tape* that illustrate ways people intimidate us. After each segment, I'll stop the tape so you and your partner can discuss how you would respond. Be ready to share your responses with the class.**

Play "Bully Buster" from the *cassette tape*. When the narrator prompts you, stop the tape and give pairs a minute to discuss how they'd respond. Sound the *squeaker* and wait until kids stop what they're doing, raise their hands, and focus on you. Have one person from each pair report their thoughts to the class.

After the third cassette segment, have one partner in each pair read **Psalm 124** and the other summarize it in one sentence. Then have pairs discuss these questions. Write them on newsprint for kids to refer to during discussions. Ask:

◆ **What was your initial response to these tape segments? Explain.** (They made me mad because I hate it when people are mean; they made me want to come up with good ideas; I was frustrated because I didn't know how to respond.)

◆ **In what ways do people intimidate you?** (They tell me I'm not good enough; they threaten to beat me up; they make fun of me.)

◆ **How do you respond?** (I get my friends to help me; I tell a teacher or my parents; I ignore it; I go away.)

◆ **When have you felt like the writer of Psalm 124?** (At school when an older kid rescued me from a bully; at home when my mom made my sister stop picking on me.)

◆ **In what ways can God help you deal with people who intimidate you like God helped the writer of Psalm 124?** (God can give me courage to face bullies; God can give me wisdom to know when to stand and when to run; God can change other people's attitudes.)

◆ **What can you do this week to help you rely on God for help in intimidating situations?** (Pray; read my Bible; sing worship songs to myself when I'm scared.)

Sound the *squeaker* to regain kids' attention. After everyone responds by raising their hands and focusing on you, have partners take turns sharing their responses to the questions.

Then say: **Sometimes when others intimidate us, it feels like we're all alone. But, as Psalm 124 reminds us, God is on our side in times of trouble, and ✍ God can help us face people who intimidate us.**

Right now, think of a time when you felt afraid, threatened, or intimidated, and God helped you out. (Pause.) **Now, silently tell God thanks for helping both you and the writer of Psalm 124.**

Give kids about 30 seconds for their silent prayers before moving to the next activity.

☜ THE **POINT**

BLOW ME DOWN! 📖

(10 to 15 minutes)

Use masking tape to mark a 6×6-foot square on the floor and divide the square into four equal sections. Place all the *flippers* of each color in separate sections of the square.

Form four teams (a team can be one person) and assign each team a color that corresponds with the *flippers*—red, green, yellow, or blue. Have each team gather around the section that contains the *flippers* that correspond to that team's colors.

Say: **The object of the game is to blow the opposing teams' *flippers* out of their sections while keeping your own *flippers* in your section. You can't touch the *flippers*, so keep your hands behind your back during the game. You have two minutes. Go!**

LEARNING LAB

TEACHER TIP

If there are more than 16 students in your class, you may want to consider making two or three squares, then dividing the *flippers* and teams between the squares.

TEACHER TIP

If you have a group of three, have one group member fill two roles. If you have a group of five, have two group members act as encouragers. Be sure to provide paper and pencils for the recorders in each group.

Sound the *squeaker* after two minutes to end the game and wait for kids to raise their hands and focus on you. If you have time, you may want to have kids switch places and play another round. After the game, collect the *flippers* for later use.

Have kids choose partners from the opposing teams to form groups of no more than four. Tell groups to assign one person to be a recorder who writes down their ideas, a second to act as a representative who shares their ideas with the class, a third to act as a reader who reads the Bible passages, and a fourth to be an encourager who urges everyone to participate in the discussion.

Ask groups to discuss the following questions:

◆ **What kinds of emotions did you experience during this activity?** (I felt like everyone was ganging up on me; I kept looking for ways to help my teammates; I wanted to protect my *flippers*.)

◆ **What was easy or difficult about this activity?** (It was hard to pay attention to both my *flippers* and the other teams' *flippers*; it was easy to blow the *flippers* out of the square when we ganged up on other teams' members.)

◆ **How was playing this game like how a bully might act?** (A bully gets in your face; he or she gets others to gang up on you; a bully is usually full of hot air.)

◆ **How was the way we ganged up on each other like the way we sometimes bully each other without realizing it?** (We get competitive and do anything to win; we forget to care about others and treat them with respect; we follow the crowd and pick on unpopular people.)

After a few minutes, sound the *squeaker* to end the small-group discussions. After everyone has responded by raising their hands and focusing on you, have the representatives take turns telling how their groups responded.

Next, have groups read **Matthew 5:43-48** and **1 Thessalonians 5:15-16.** Tell kids to look for advice from these passages on how to deal with a bully. Have the recorders write the advice on a sheet of paper. Have the representatives report their groups' advice to the class. Kids might say things like "Pray for the bully," "Treat the bully like you want to be treated," or "Don't look for ways to get even."

Have kids stand as you ask the following questions. Give kids a few seconds to think after each question and tell them you'd like to hear lots of interesting responses. When one student shares an answer, he or she—and anyone who thought of the same answer and has nothing more to add—can sit down. When all kids are seated, ask the next question and repeat the process.

TEACHER TIP

If all kids sit down after the first student shares an answer, have kids stand up. Then ask the question again to encourage another response.

Ask:

◆ **How did our actions during the game compare to the advice of these passages?** (We were all playing against each other instead of being kind; we were looking out only for ourselves instead of for others.)

◆ **Why do you think the Bible encourages us to be nice to people who are mean to us?** (Because it shows God's love to others; because it can make a friend out of an enemy.)

◆ **What makes it difficult for you to follow the advice of these Scriptures?** (I'm scared a bully might really hurt me; I get so mad about the way bullies treat me.)

◆ **What techniques can we use to make it easier for us to follow the advice of these Scriptures without putting ourselves in danger?** (Ask a teacher or parent for help; talk over the problem with the bully; give a strong verbal message like "Stop that.")

Sound the *squeaker* to end the small-group discussions. After everyone has responded by raising their hands and focusing on you, have the representatives take turns reporting their answers to the class.

Say: **Although following the advice of Matthew 5:43-48 and 1 Thessalonians 5:15-16 isn't easy, it is one way God can help us face people who intimidate us this week.**

🦅 THE **POINT**

BULLY SHIELD 📖

(7 to 12 minutes)

If you skipped the previous activity, form groups of no more than four. Give each person a sheet of paper and a pencil.

Say: **Your group has just been hired as self-defense instructors. You have new recruits coming in who need training to help protect themselves from bullies. Your first assignment is to draw a shield on your paper.** (Pause.) **Now, come up with tactics your recruits can use to protect themselves and write them on your shields.**

For example, you might instruct your students to use strong verbal messages like "Don't touch me!" or you might tell them to pray. Think of other tactics to include on your shields. Be ready to share your ideas with the class. You have two minutes. Go.

Sound the *squeaker* after two minutes to call everyone together. After kids have responded by raising their hands and focusing on you, have the person wearing the most red in each group report his or her group's ideas. Encourage everyone to add the new ideas they hear to their own shields.

Then have groups discuss these questions one at a time. Have the oldest person in each group share answers to the first question, next oldest share answers to the second question, and so on. Ask:

◆ **As self-defense instructors, how did you feel about creating your bully shields?** (I felt good knowing it could help others; I was worried our ideas wouldn't work.)

◆ **Why do you think it might be important to know tactics you can use to protect yourselves?** (So you're prepared for situations where people pick on you; to help you calm your fears; so you can stop people from bullying you.)

Have the youngest person in each group read **Psalm 3:3-6** aloud. Have others in the group summarize the passage in one sentence. On their shields, have kids write their groups' summaries. Then ask:

◆ **In what ways is God a shield for us?** (God can stop others from intimidating us; God gives us courage to face bullies; God can help us overcome our fears.)

◆ **How can God use the ideas on our bully shields to protect us?** (God can answer our prayers about bullies; God can remind us to get help from a parent or teacher; God can give us courage to give strong verbal messages.)

◆ **What can we do this week to help us trust God to shield us from intimidating people?** (Pray for God's help; remind each other about **Psalm 3:3-6;** encourage each other to trust God.)

THE POINT ☞

Say: ☞ **God can help us face people who intimidate us when we trust in him for protection. Take your shields home as a reminder that God is our ultimate shield when we must face bullies.**

TABLE™ TENT

We believe Christian education extends beyond the classroom into the home. Photocopy the "Table Tent" handout (p. 22) for this week and send it home with your kids. Encourage kids and parents to use the handout to spark meaningful discussion on this week's topic. Follow up next week by asking kids how their discussions went with their families.

CLOSING

THREE CHEERS FOR US

(5 to 10 minutes)

Form pairs and have partners take turns answering this question: **What's one important thing you learned today?** (God can help us face people who intimidate us; even though bullies are mean to us, we can respond to them with kindness; God can help us shield ourselves from bully troubles.)

Sound the *squeaker* to regain kids' attention. After kids respond by raising their hands and focusing on you, have groups report their answers to the class.

Next, form two teams—team A and team B—and say: **One way God can help us face people who intimidate us is by giving us encouragement from our friends. I want all of us to be encouraging friends to each other, so let's practice that now by doing the activity "Three Cheers for Us."**

Place the *mini straw hat* on the head of a student in team A. Tell kids the object of this game is to cheer each member of the other team. The game is played in rounds of competing cheers. Taking turns, each team cheers, "(Student's name, student's name)! We're going to be good friends for (student's name)!"

Have each team fill in the blanks with the name of the person wearing the *mini straw hat,* then give the hat to a new person on the opposite team after each cheer. For example, team B might start the cheering by yelling, "Bob, Bob! We're going to be good friends for Bob!" Then team A would place the *mini straw hat* on the head of one of team B's members and cheer for that person.

Decide at the end of each round which team cheered the loudest. Continue until all students have been cheered. Then dismiss with applause for everyone.

LEARNING LAB

 THE POINT

TEACHER TIP

The activity "Three Cheers for Us" is adapted from the book *Esteem Builders for Children's Ministry,* available from Group Publishing. Check it out for over 100 practical ideas on how to build confident kids.

TEACHER TIP

If your class' cheering would disturb other classes, try having kids cheer in their loudest whispers.

TABLE™
TENT

"Our help comes from the Lord, who made heaven and earth"
(Psalm 124:8).

Talk Triggers

▲ What intimidates you the most (or makes you most afraid)? Why?

▲ Why do you think people become bullies? How should a person deal with bullies?

THE WORD on Bullies

Monday   Romans 12:20-21
How can we overcome evil with good?

Tuesday   Ephesians 6:13-18
Which part of God's armor do you think is the best protection from a bully? Why?

Wednesday   1 Corinthians 13:4-7
Do you think you could act lovingly toward someone who is bullying you? Why or why not?

Thursday   Mark 15:1-20
Why did God allow Jesus to suffer at the hands of bullies? Why does God allow people to suffer because of bullies today?

Friday   Matthew 28:20b
How can Jesus be with you when you must face a bully?

Saturday   Psalm 121
How can this passage encourage you as you face intimidating situations?

NEVER-ENDING BLUES?

THE POINT

☞ **God cares when we're feeling down.**

THE BIBLE BASIS

Psalm 34:17-19

> The Lord hears good people when they cry out to him, and he saves them from all their troubles. The Lord is close to the brokenhearted, and he saves those whose spirits have been crushed. People who do what is right may have many problems, but the Lord will solve them all.

David reigned as king over all of Israel, so surely he never battled depression, right? Wrong. Wars, family problems, and personal failings repeatedly plagued King David's life. Many of the psalms he wrote reflect a man in despair. Yet, in spite of discouraging circumstances, David refused to give up hope because "the Lord is close to the brokenhearted."

Many of today's fifth- and sixth-graders can be counted among the brokenhearted. Depression affects up to 33 percent of adolescents. Suicide rates among 10- to 14-year-olds have nearly tripled since 1968.

Because kids have yet to fully experience the ups and downs of life, they can sometimes feel that depression will never end. They need to know that God can, and will, help them through depressing times. Other Scriptures used in the lesson are **Philippians 4:6; Jeremiah 15:16; Matthew 11:28-30; and Matthew 26:36-46.**

GETTING THE POINT

Students will
◆ talk about what makes them feel depressed,
◆ participate in a relay of depression-busting activities,
◆ examine the story of Jesus in the garden of Gethsemane, and
◆ experience laughter.

THIS LESSON AT A GLANCE

SECTION	MINUTES	WHAT STUDENTS WILL DO	LEARNING LAB SUPPLIES	CLASSROOM SUPPLIES
ATTENTION GRABBER	5 to 10	**Stomp It**—Stomp, crush, and squish a piece of newspaper.		Newspaper
BIBLE EXPLORATION AND APPLICATION	9 to 14	**Now That's Depressing**—Pantomime depressing situations and discuss Psalm 34:17-19.	Mini straw hat, twirlybird, elastic strips	Bibles, newsprint, markers
	9 to 14	**Depression-Buster Relay**—Practice techniques for beating depression and talk about Psalm 34:17; Philippians 4:6; Jeremiah 15:16; and Matthew 11:28-30.	Mini straw hat, twirlybird, flippers, squeaker	Bibles, newsprint, marker
	7 to 12	**In the Garden**—Examine Matthew 26:36-46 and practice encouraging each other.	Cassette: "In the Garden"	Bibles, cassette player, newsprint, marker, paper, pencils
CLOSING	5 to 10	**Laugh It Up**—Laugh!		

Remember to make photocopies of the "Table Tent" handout (p. 32) to send home with your kids. The "Table Tent" is a valuable tool for helping fifth- and sixth-graders talk with their parents about what they're learning in class.

THE LESSON

Before the lesson, collect the necessary items from the Learning Lab for the activities you plan to use. Refer to the pictures in the margins to see what each item looks like.

As kids arrive, ask them about last week's "Table Tent" discussion. Use questions such as "What did you learn about your family?" and "What surprised you about your family's reactions?" However, be careful not to embarrass students whose families choose not to use the "Table Tent."

ATTENTION GRABBER

STOMP IT

(5 to 10 minutes)

Begin class with a reminder to kids that whenever you sound the *squeaker,* they're to stop what they're doing, raise their hands, and focus on you. Practice the signal two or three times. Then give a sheet of newspaper to each student.

Say: **You have one minute to stomp on, squish, smash, and crush this piece of newspaper. The object is to get your piece of newspaper as small as you can. When you hear the *squeaker,* time's up. Ready? Go!**

After one minute, call time by sounding the *squeaker.* When kids have responded by raising their hands and focusing on you, say: **Let's see how you did. Hold up your newspapers.**

Inspect the newspapers to see who was able to make theirs the smallest. Then form a circle and ask:

◆ **What were you thinking during this activity?** (All I could think about was crushing my paper; I felt like I was venting frustration; I wanted to make sure mine was the smallest.)

◆ **When have you felt "stomped on" or "crushed" by circumstances?** (When I got a bad grade in science class; when one of my relatives died.)

◆ **What do you do when you feel depressed or discouraged?** (I cry a lot; I just want to be alone; I eat chocolate; I pray; I talk to a friend.)

Hold up the smallest piece of crushed newspaper and say: **Sometimes life leaves us feeling like this newspaper—crushed, stomped on, and depressed. The good news is that  God cares when we're feeling down. So, today we're going to learn what to do when we're feeling discouraged.**

LEARNING LAB

TEACHER TIP

Encourage active participation as students report back by following up kids' answers with questions such as "What did you mean by that?" and "Can you tell me more?"

It's important to say The Point just as it's written in each activity. Repeating The Point over and over throughout the lesson will help kids remember it and apply it to their lives.

 THE **POINT**

BIBLE EXPLORATION AND APPLICATION

LEARNING LAB

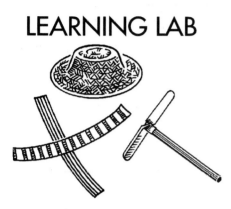

TEACHER TIP

If you have more than 12 students in class, you may want to have kids prepare and perform their pantomimes in foursomes. Also, you may want to limit performances to no more than 30 seconds each.

Tell kids who use the *twirlybird* to remember these safety precautions:

◆ always spin the *twirlybird* in a counterclockwise direction and

◆ don't aim the *twirlybird* at anyone's face or eyes (including your own).

NOW THAT'S DEPRESSING

(9 to 14 minutes)

Form pairs and say: **Tell your partners one or two things that make you feel depressed. For example, you might mention a friend moving away, flunking a homework assignment, or disappointing your parents.**

Give kids about one minute to talk, then sound the *squeaker* to regain students' attention. Wait for kids to respond by stopping what they're doing, raising their hands, and focusing on you.

Say: **Now choose one of the things you and your partner talked about and prepare a pantomime to illustrate it. You'll have two minutes to prepare, and you can use the *mini straw hat*, the *twirlybird*, or the *elastic strips* as props if you wish.**

Sound the *squeaker* after two minutes to end preparations and wait for kids to respond. Have pairs take turns performing their pantomimes for the class while other students try to guess what's being acted out. Lead kids in applauding all performers.

Afterward, have one partner in each pair read **Psalm 34:17-19** and the other summarize it in one sentence. Then have pairs discuss the following questions. Write the questions on newsprint for kids to refer to during discussions. Tell kids to be ready to share new insights they gain. Ask:

◆ **What was easy or difficult for you about this activity?** (It was easy to think of things that depress me; it was hard to act out exactly how a situation makes me feel depressed.)

◆ **Why do the things you acted out make you feel depressed?** (Because they mean I've failed somehow; because they make me feel out of control.)

◆ **Why do you think so many people are affected by depression?** (Because everybody has good days and bad days; because everyone wants to be successful and popular.)

◆ **How could Psalm 34:17-19 encourage you when you're in a situation like the ones we pantomimed?** (It could remind me that God cares; it could help me tell God how I'm feeling; it can give me hope that God will work everything out.)

◆ **Why do you think God cares when we're feeling "brokenhearted" or depressed?** (Because we're God's children; because God loves us; because God wants the best for us.)

◆ **How can God help us overcome depression?** (By reminding us that God loves us; by giving us a friend to talk to; by showing us an encouraging Scripture like **Psalm 34:17-19.**)

◆ **How can we help others this week who may be feeling brokenhearted or depressed?** (Say or do something encouraging for them; listen when they cry; be available for them; tell them about **Psalm 34:17-19;** pray for them.)

Sound the *squeaker* to end discussions. When kids respond by raising their hands and focusing on you, have pairs take turns sharing new insights they gained from their discussions.

Say: **Everyone goes through depressing times, and that's OK. Life will always have its ups and downs. However, we can be encouraged because Psalm 34:17-19 makes it clear that** ☞ **God cares when we're feeling down.**

THE **POINT**

LEARNING LAB

TEACHER TIP

This is a great activity to do outside, if weather permits.

DEPRESSION-BUSTER RELAY

(9 to 14 minutes)

Designate six stations around the room. Write the following directions on separate sheets of newsprint and place the appropriate directions and supplies at the corresponding stations.

Station 1: "Get Rest"—Lie on the floor and snore for 30 seconds.

Station 2: "Help Others"—Kindly help an elderly person to his or her chair (group members take turns wearing the *mini straw hat* and pretending to be elderly).

Station 3: "Count Your Blessings"—As a group, take turns naming things you're grateful for, such as your family, friends, teachers, church, or holidays. Name as many as you can in 30 seconds.

Station 4: "Pray"—Take turns saying this prayer: Lord, when I'm feeling rotten, remind me that I can talk to you about it. In Jesus' name, amen.

Station 5: "Read the Bible"—Read aloud **Psalm 34:17-19** in unison.

Station 6: "Do Something Just for Fun"—Just for fun, take turns spinning the *twirlybird* and flipping the *flippers*.

Form groups of no more than four and say: **There are many ways God can help us overcome depression. Let's** practice a few of them right now in a depression-buster relay.

Have groups stand at different stations to begin. If you have over 24 students, it's OK to have more than one group at a station.

Say: **When I sound the *squeaker,* that'll be your cue to begin the relay by following the direction on the newsprint at your station. You'll have 30 seconds at each station. I'll sound the *squeaker* when it's time to move to the next station. After you've been to all six stations, we'll gather in the center of the room. Ready? Go.**

Lead kids through the relay. Show groups by example that it's OK to have fun during the relay. After kids have been to all six stations, form a circle in the center of the room.

Have kids stand as you ask the following questions. When one student shares an answer, have anyone who thought of the same answer and has nothing more to add take a step backward. When everyone has stepped back, ask the next question and repeat the process.

◆ **What did you like best about this relay? Why?** (Twirling the *twirlybird* because it was fun; taking a nap because I was tired; reading the Scripture verse because it reminded me that God cares.)

◆ **How could God use the techniques in the depression-buster relay to help you get over a depressing time in real life?** (God could encourage us with a Bible verse; God could encourage us to do something fun to take our minds off our depression; God could remind us of all the positive things in our lives.)

◆ **What are some other ways God could encourage you during a depressing time?** (By having a friend listen to me; by having my parents give me a hug; by reminding me that God cares.)

Re-form the groups of no more than four. Have group members designate one person to be red, one to be blue, one to be green, and one to be purple.

Assign the reds **Psalm 34:17,** the blues **Philippians 4:4-7,** the greens **Jeremiah 15:16,** and the purples **Matthew 11:28-30.** Have group members take turns reading their assigned passages aloud to each other. Then re-form the circle and ask these questions:

◆ **How are these verses similar to what we did in our depression-buster relay?** (We prayed in the relay like **Psalm 34:17** and **Philippians 4:6** encourage us to; we read the Bible like Jeremiah did; we rested the way Jesus promises rest in **Matthew 11:28-30.**)

◆ **What makes it hard for you to follow the advice of**

TEACHER TIP

Here are a few guidelines to encourage dialogue as you ask questions:

◆ Give kids a few seconds to think after each question and tell them you'd like to hear lots of interesting responses.

◆ If all kids step back after the first student shares an answer, have kids re-form the circle. Then ask the question again to encourage another response.

◆ Let your kids know that all answers are welcome. Communicate a policy of "no wrong answers."

◆ If kids respond with "I don't know," ask, "If you did know, what would your answer be?"

these Scriptures when you're depressed? (I don't feel like doing anything when I'm depressed; when I'm depressed it doesn't seem like God or anyone else cares.)

◆ **What have you learned from these Scriptures or from the relay that can help you through depressing times this week?** (I can tell God my troubles because God cares; I can try one of the activities from the depression-buster relay when I'm feeling down.)

◆ **What's one thing you can do this week to help your friends when they may be feeling down?** (I can listen; I can offer help in solving a problem; I can pray; I can help them focus on the good things in their lives.)

Say: 🖘God cares when we're feeling down, and God can help us overcome depression in a variety of ways. This week, remember the advice of our Scriptures and the activities we did in our relay to help you get past depressed feelings.

🖘 THE **POINT**

IN THE GARDEN 📖

LEARNING LAB

(7 to 12 minutes)

Form groups of no more than three and give each group a sheet of paper and a pencil. Have groups assign the following roles within their trios: one person to be a recorder who writes down the group's thoughts, one person to act as a representative who shares the group's thoughts with the class, and one person to act as an encourager who urges everyone to participate in the discussion.

Say: **Depression isn't something new. As a matter of fact, Jesus himself dealt with depression 2,000 years ago. Let's listen to this dramatization based on Matthew 26:36-46, which tells the story of a time when Jesus faced depression.**

Play "In The Garden" from the *cassette tape.* As groups are listening to the *cassette tape,* write the next set of questions on newsprint for kids to refer to. When the segment is finished, have kids discuss these questions in their groups. Ask:

◆ **How does it make you feel to hear about Jesus' struggle through a depressing time?** (Weird because it's hard to imagine him being depressed; grateful because he knows what I feel like; sad because he had to go through that.)

◆ **What's your opinion of Jesus' friends after hearing this story? Why?** (I feel sorry for them because they missed a chance to help Jesus; I think they should have been better friends to him and stayed awake.)

◆ **What do you think Jesus' friends could've done to encourage him?** (Stayed awake; prayed with him; talked with him; hugged him.)

◆ **How does God use friends or family members to encourage you when you're depressed?** (My best friend always listens when I have a problem; my dad takes me out for ice cream to cheer me up.)

◆ **What can you do this week to be the kind of friend or family member God uses to encourage others when they're down?** (Send a card to a friend; make dinner for my family; help my brother do his homework; invite a friend to do something fun.)

After a few minutes, sound the *squeaker* to end the small-group discussions. After everyone has responded by raising their hands and focusing on you, have the representatives take turns reporting their group's thoughts to the class.

Say: **Although Jesus' friends left him to deal with his depression alone, we can always count on the fact that ☞ God cares when we're feeling down.**

THE POINT ☞

Often, God will send a friend or a family member to encourage us when we're down. And, we can be a friend or family member that God uses to encourage others. Let's do a quick activity to practice being God's encouragers.

Form a circle and say: **When I call out an object that everyone can see, let's all run to it and cheer it up with compliments, a joke, a prayer, applause, a quotation from Scripture or whatever you can think of. Return to your place in the circle when I sound the *squeaker.***

Choose one thing on each student to be "cheered up," such as Sarah's red sweater, John's baseball cap, or Mary's watch. End the activity when something on everyone has been "cheered up."

Gather everyone around and say: **Everyone needs a little cheering up sometimes. This week, let's be the kind of friends and family members who show others with our actions that ☞ God cares when we're feeling down.**

THE POINT ☞

CLOSING

LAUGH IT UP

(5 to 10 minutes)

Line kids up alphabetically based on the first letter of their last name. Ask kids the following question, then have them shout out the answer in unison: **What was The Point of today's lesson?** (God cares when we're feeling down.)

Say: **Sometimes laughter is the best medicine when we're feeling down. I'll show you what I mean.**

Have the first person in line lie down on the floor on his or her back. Then have the next person in line lie down with his or her head on the first person's stomach. Continue having kids lie down until everyone is lying with his or her head on someone else's stomach.

Say: **The first person begins this game by saying "Ha." The next person says, "Ha ha." The third person says "Ha ha ha," and so on. Now, this is a very *serious* game (ha ha). If anyone starts laughing, the game begins again with the first person.**

Kids will have a hard time waiting their turn to say "Ha," but that's OK. This game is actually designed solely to get everyone laughing.

After the class has had a good laugh, end the game and say: **This week, let's remember to encourage each other with the news that**  **God cares when we're feeling down.**

TEACHER TIP

Depending on the maturity level of your class, you may want to form a line of boys and a line of girls instead of having the entire class form one line.

🖎 **THE POINT**

"The Lord hears good people when they cry out to him, and he saves them from all their troubles" (Psalm 34:17).

Talk Triggers

◆ How would you define "depression"? What makes you feel depressed?

◆ Tell about a time when you were depressed and how you got over it.

THE WORD on Depression

Monday   Matthew 11:28-30
What things weigh on your heart like heavy loads? How can you turn those things over to Jesus?

Tuesday   Luke 18:1-8
When have you felt hopeless? What did you do?

Wednesday   Philippians 4:6-7
What part does worry play in depression? How can God's peace help you overcome depression?

Thursday   1 Kings 19:1-18
How can you find God's quiet voice when you're feeling down?

Friday   James 1:2-4
What's the difference between being joyful *in* trials and being joyful *for* trials? How can we be joyful in any circumstance?

Saturday   Matthew 26:38
How does it make you feel to know that Jesus was overwhelmed with sorrow? Why?

Even life in the circus has its depressing moments.

(fold here)

(fold here)

DEALING WITH FAMILY CRISES

THE POINT

☞ **God can heal hurting families.**

THE BIBLE BASIS

Psalm 23

The Lord is my shepherd; I have everything I need. He lets me rest in green pastures. He leads me to calm water. He gives me new strength. He leads me on paths that are right for the good of his name. Even if I walk through a very dark valley, I will not be afraid, because you are with me. Your rod and your walking stick comfort me.

You prepare a meal for me in front of my enemies. You pour oil on my head; you fill my cup to overflowing. Surely your goodness and love will be with me all my life, and I will live in the house of the Lord forever.

One of the best-known Scriptures in the Bible, **Psalm 23,** reaffirms God's love for us. In beautiful prose, David describes God as a shepherd who cares for, protects, encourages, and safely leads his sheep through the "dark valleys" of life.

For fifth- and sixth-graders, the dark valleys of life often come in the form of family crises. Allie's mother loses her job, straining the family's budget and patience with each other. Jim's parents are divorcing, planting seeds of bitterness within him. Kiesha's dad has been offered a job in another state, meaning the whole family must move.

Use this lesson to show your Allies, Jims, and Kieshas that God, the Good Shepherd, will care for them when they must walk through the dark valleys of family crises. Other Scriptures used in the lesson are **Job 1–2:13; Job 42:12-17;** and **Galatians 6:2.**

GETTING THE POINT

Students will
◆ discuss how God cares for hurting families like a shepherd watches over his sheep,
◆ examine families in the Bible who've faced crises, and
◆ compare working together in a game to working together during family crises.

THIS LESSON AT A GLANCE

SECTION	MINUTES	WHAT STUDENTS WILL DO	LEARNING LAB SUPPLIES	CLASSROOM SUPPLIES
ATTENTION GRABBER	5 to 10	**People Pileup**—Compare how family troubles pile up to a piling-up game.		
BIBLE EXPLORATION AND APPLICATION	10 to 15	**Sheep and Shepherds**—Discuss Psalm 23 after pretending to be a family of sheep.	Cassette: "Thy Word," lyrics poster	Bibles, "Sheep and Shepherds" handout (p. 42), newsprint, masking tape, snacks, cassette player
	8 to 13	**Advice for the Past**—Offer advice to Job and his wife, then examine Psalm 23:1-4; Job 1–2:13; and Job 42:12-17.	Cassette: "Family Crisis"	Bibles, cassette player, paper, pencils
	7 to 12	**Catch the Twirlybird**—Compare working together to catch a twirlybird to working together to overcome family crises and talk about Galatians 6:2.	Twirlybird	Bibles, newsprint, marker
CLOSING	5 to 10	**Twirlybird Encouragements**—Practice being encouraging family members.	Twirlybird	

Remember to make photocopies of the "Table Tent" handout (p. 43) to send home with your kids. The "Table Tent" is a valuable tool for helping fifth- and sixth-graders talk with their parents about what they're learning in class.

THE LESSON

Before the lesson, collect the necessary items from the Learning Lab for the activities you plan to use. Refer to the pictures in the margins to see what each item looks like.

As kids arrive, ask them about last week's "Table Tent" discussion. Use questions such as "What did you learn about your family?" and "What surprised you about your family's reactions?" However, be careful not to embarrass students whose families choose not to use the "Table Tent."

ATTENTION GRABBER

PEOPLE PILEUP

(5 to 10 minutes)

Begin class with a reminder to kids that whenever you sound the *squeaker,* they're to stop what they're doing, raise their hands, and focus on you. Practice the signal two or three times.

Form a circle and have each student sit in a chair.

Say: **We'll begin today with a quick game called People Pileup. During this game, you may wind up on someone else's lap, and others may wind up on yours, so be careful not to smash anyone. Follow the instructions as I read them.**

Read the following list of instructions and have kids move accordingly.

Instructions

◆ If you're an only child, move two places to your left.

◆ If you know of a family that's gone through a divorce, move three places to your right.

◆ If you had an argument with a family member in the past week, move one space to the right.

◆ If you had an argument with a family member today, move two spaces to the right.

◆ If someone in your family has ever lost a job, move three places to your left.

◆ If someone in your family ever spent the night in a hospital, move two spaces to the left.

◆ If your family has ever moved to another state, move one space to the right.

◆ If you've lived in three different states or outside the United States, move four spaces to the right.

TEACHER TIP

Depending on the maturity level of your class, you may want to form a circle of boys and a circle of girls instead of having the entire class form one circle.

TEACHER TIP

It's important to say The Point just as it's written in each activity. Repeating The Point over and over throughout the lesson will help kids remember it and apply it to their lives.

THE **POINT**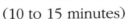

LEARNING LAB

TEACHER TIP

If you must form a group of five, have two students act as shepherds. If you have a group of three, have that group eliminate the role of the middle sheep.

End the game and have kids return to their seats in the circle. Ask:

◆ **What were you thinking as we played this game?** (I wondered if I would ever get out from under the pile; I was surprised at how often I had to move; I hoped no one would sit on me.)

◆ **How can family problems "pile up" on us like we piled up on each other during this game?** (Family problems can make us feel crushed; family problems can make it hard for us to get along with each other.)

◆ **What problems or changes must families deal with from time to time?** (A parent loses a job; the family moves; a new baby is born; someone in the family is addicted to drugs or alcohol.)

Say: **Problems cause pain in every family, and your family is no exception. But, your family can take heart because the Bible teaches that** **God can heal hurting families. Let's explore this more.**

BIBLE EXPLORATION AND APPLICATION

SHEEP AND SHEPHERDS

(10 to 15 minutes)

Photocopy and cut apart the "Sheep and Shepherds" handout on page 42. Make sure you have enough roles for each group member to have one. Roll up newsprint and tape the ends to form "staffs" for the shepherds. You'll need one staff for every four students.

Form groups of no more than four and have groups stand at one end of the room. Set out snacks such as fruit or doughnuts at the other end of the room.

Say: **Your group is a family of sheep. Right now, designate one person in your group to be a shepherd, one to be the oldest sheep, one to be the middle sheep, and one to be the baby lamb.**

Pause while kids assign their roles. Then hand out the instructions that correspond with each role. Caution kids not to let others read their instructions.

Say: **Your roles for this activity are explained on the instructions I gave you. Even though you're a family of** sheep, don't be afraid to "ham up" your roles. Shepherds, you've got two minutes to lead your family of sheep to the snacks and back. I'll sound the *squeaker* when two minutes are up. Go.

Sound the *squeaker* to end the activity. After kids respond by raising their hands and focusing on you, ask:

◆ **What were you thinking during this activity?** (I couldn't figure out how to get my family of sheep together; I missed my family of sheep; I wanted the shepherd to help me so I could get a snack.)

Say: **Discuss the next few questions in your groups. Then I'll call out one of the roles. The person in your group who played that role will be responsible for sharing your group's answer.**

Ask:

◆ **What was easy or difficult for you in this activity? Why?** (It was hard being the shepherd because each of my sheep was doing something different; it was easy because all I had to do was what my shepherd said.)

◆ **How is the way our sheep families split up like the way family crises divide our homes?** (We cry for attention during a hard time; we assume our parents will take care of the problem, so we just do our own thing.)

◆ **What do you do when something big changes or seems to go wrong in your family?** (I pray about it; I worry; I try to help out in any way I can; I feel like it's my fault.)

Have the shepherds in each group read **Psalm 23** aloud. Then have all the sheep summarize the theme of the passage in one sentence. Have the baby lambs take turns sharing their groups' summaries with the class. Afterward, have the class discuss these questions:

◆ **How were the shepherds in our activity like or unlike God, the Good Shepherd described in Psalm 23?** (Like God, our shepherds wanted to take care of their sheep; unlike God, our shepherds lost control.)

◆ **How can God be a shepherd to us when our families are going through a rough time?** (God can help us feel better in spite of our circumstances; God can change our attitudes; God can help us feel loved and cared for.)

◆ **A shepherd uses a staff to guide sheep out of dangerous and unpleasant circumstances. What does God use to guide us through painful family crises?** (The Bible; other family members; prayer; our church; positive attitudes; encouraging friends.)

◆ **What can you do this week to help you and your family trust God, the Good Shepherd, during painful times?** (I can remind my family members about **Psalm 23;** I

TEACHER TIP

Encourage active participation as students report back by following up kids' answers with questions such as "What did you mean by that?" and "Can you tell me more?"

can think about ways God has cared for my family in the past;
I can read the Bible.)

Say: **Family crises can often make us feel like lost and
afraid sheep without a shepherd. But God is the Good
Shepherd, and  God can heal hurting families. In
times of trouble, your family can take confidence in
knowing God is with you.**

Show kids the words to the song "Thy Word," written on
the *lyrics poster*. Have kids think of a time when a family
problem made them feel afraid or confused like the author of
the song.

Then say: **One great resource God uses to heal hurting
families is the Bible. Let's learn a new song that will remind us to turn to the Bible during our next family crisis.**

Teach kids the song "Thy Word." Use the *cassette tape* and
lyrics poster to assist you.

THE **POINT**

LEARNING LAB

ADVICE FOR THE PAST

(8 to 13 minutes)

If you skipped the previous activity, form groups of no
more than four. Tell groups to assign the following roles within their foursomes: one person to be a recorder who writes
down the group's thoughts, one person to act as a representative who shares the group's thoughts with the class, one person to act as a reader who'll read the Scriptures, and one person to be an encourager who urges everyone to participate in
the discussion.

Say: **We're going to listen to a cassette segment about
a family in crisis. Afterward, I'd like your group to discuss what advice you'd give to the people involved. We'll
take turns reporting our advice to the class.**

Play "Family Crisis" from the *cassette tape*. Stop the tape
after the segment for group discussion. Be sure the recorders
in each group have paper and pencils. Have the representatives each report their group's advice after the segment.

After kids have given advice for Job, have the readers read
Job 2:11-13 to find out what happened next in the story.
Then have groups discuss the following questions:

◆ **How does it make you feel to know that families in
the Bible had problems? Explain.** (Encouraged, because
that means my family doesn't have to be perfect; worried,
because if things could go wrong for them, they could go
wrong for me, too.)

◆ **What feelings do you think Job's family experienced**

that people going through a family crisis today might feel? (Sadness; disappointment; anger; jealousy; confusion.)

◆ **How does this family crisis from the Bible compare to family crises today?** (I know someone who's really sick like Job was; my uncle lost all his money and his job like Job did.)

Sound the *squeaker* to end small-group discussions. After everyone has responded by raising their hands and focusing on you, have the representatives report their groups' answers. Next, have the readers read **Psalm 23:1-4** aloud and in unison for the class. Then have kids discuss these questions:

◆ **How might this passage have encouraged Job and his wife?** (It could've reminded them that God cared; it could've encouraged them to trust God; it could've reminded them that God would be with them.)

◆ **How might this passage encourage you during a family crisis?** (It could help me not be afraid; it could remind me I'm important to God; it could show me I'm never alone.)

◆ **Based on Psalm 23:1-4, what advice could you give yourself the next time you face a family crisis?** (Trust God to help you through this time; ask God to help you overcome your fears; tell your family about the encouragement of **Psalm 23**.)

After a few minutes of discussion, sound the *squeaker* again and wait for kids to respond. Have kids read aloud **Job 42:12-17** to find out how Job's family crisis ended.

Then say: **Just as God helped Job and his wife long ago, God can heal hurting families today.**

Think of a family you know of that's going through a crisis right now. It may be your family or someone else's. (Pause.) **Let's spend a minute praying silently for God to help the families we thought of as they deal with their problems this week.**

Have kids spend a minute in silent prayer before moving on to the next activity.

✍ THE **POINT**

CATCH THE TWIRLYBIRD

LEARNING LAB

(7 to 12 minutes)

Form two teams. Have team members hold hands to form two circles, then have the circles stand on opposite ends of the room.

Stand in the center of the room and show kids the *twirlybird*.

THE **POINT** 🖝

Say: **The object of this game is to make the *twirlybird* land inside your circle when I spin it into the air. You can move around the room to get under the *twirlybird*, but everyone in your circle must always hold hands. Each team will have three turns. Let's see if we can catch it every time.**

Choose a team to go first. Spin the *twirlybird* in the air toward them. If they make it land easily within their circle, aim the *twirlybird* a little farther away from them the next time. Give each team three turns.

Afterward, retrieve the *twirlybird* for use in the next activity. Have kids choose a partner from the opposing team to form pairs for discussion. Tell kids to be prepared to share any new insights they gain from their discussions. Write the questions on newsprint for kids to refer to while you ask:

◆ **What was easy or difficult about this activity for you? Why?** (It was tough for all of my team to move at once; it was easy when we only had to lean over to catch the *twirlybird*.)

◆ **What helped your team succeed at this activity?** (We all worked together; we watched out for each other; we all kept focused on the *twirlybird*.)

◆ **What can we learn from this activity that could help families succeed in overcoming tough times?** (Families need to work together; family members need to watch out for each other; families need to stay focused on God.)

Have one partner in each pair read **Galatians 6:2** and the other summarize it. Then ask:

◆ **In what ways did we follow the instructions of Galatians 6:2 during our *twirlybird* activity?** (We helped each other; everyone was involved in completing the task; we encouraged each other.)

◆ **How can following the instructions of Galatians 6:2 help God heal hurting families?** (God can show us ways to help; God can use the way we work together to solve the problem; God can show us that we can do our part without complaining.)

◆ **What can you do this week to help you practice following the instructions of Galatians 6:2?** (I can write **Galatians 6:2** on my notebooks to remind me to help others; I can look for ways to help others in my family.)

Say: **One powerful way 🖝 God can heal hurting families is through family members themselves. When we all help and encourage each other, we open the doors for God to use us as part of the solution to family problems.**

CLOSING

TWIRLYBIRD ENCOURAGEMENTS

(5 to 10 minutes)

Form a circle and have kids take turns responding to this question:

◆ **What's one thing you've learned today that you'd like your friends to know?** (God can heal hurting families; God can use you to heal a hurting family; we can trust God to care for us during a family crisis.)

Say: **It's good to know that  God can heal hurting families. It's also good to know that God can use each one of us to encourage our family members during hard times. Since this class is a family of sorts, let's do a quick activity before we dismiss to practice encouraging other family members.**

Select one student to stand in the middle of the circle with the *twirlybird*. Give kids 10 seconds to think of one word that describes something positive that student would add to a family. For example, kids might mention "strength," "cheerfulness," "love," "helpfulness," and so on.

After 10 seconds, have the student in the center spin the *twirlybird* in the air. While the *twirlybird* is spinning, have the other class members take turns shouting out their descriptive words as fast as they can. See if everyone can shout out a positive word before the *twirlybird* hits the floor.

Select a new student to stand in the middle and repeat the process until everyone has had a chance to spin the *twirlybird*. Retrieve the *twirlybird* for later use before dismissing class.

LEARNING LAB

🖎 THE **POINT**

SHEEP AND SHEPHERDS

Photocopy and cut apart these roles to use during the "Sheep and Shepherds" activity. Make sure you cut apart enough roles for each student to have one.

SHEPHERD

As a shepherd, you're happiest when your sheep are well-fed, safe, and happy. Your job is to lead your family of sheep to the snacks and back. You can use your rod to help direct your sheep, but you may never hit your sheep.

Care for any sick or hurt sheep in your flock. And above all, keep your family of sheep together so they can remain safe.

OLDEST SHEEP

You like your shepherd, but you feel it's time to take charge of your own life. After all, you're the oldest. Try to find a new route to the snacks. You may even join another family of sheep just to see how they do things. Always return to your family when the shepherd calls you, but make the shepherd call you two or three times before you return. Then strike out on your own again.

MIDDLE SHEEP

You're a good sheep and like your shepherd, but now and then you become curious and want to go look at things. You don't really care about the snacks. As the shepherd leads the other sheep, find things to be curious about. Make the shepherd come get you, then follow his or her leading. Once you're back with your family, find something new to be curious about.

BABY LAMB

As a baby lamb, you're timid and easily scared. Stay as close to the shepherd as you can. However, 30 seconds into your journey, become sick or injured. Lie on the floor and "baaa" noisily whenever your shepherd isn't near you. You can only move if the shepherd helps you.

TABLE™ TENT

THE WORD on Dealing With Family Crises

Monday Revelation 21:4
What do you think it will be like to have God wipe away your tears?

Tuesday 2 Corinthians 8:1-2
When have you experienced joy while going through a hard time? How did that affect your actions?

Wednesday 1 Thessalonians 5:16-18
What makes it easy or difficult for you to follow the advice of this Scripture during a family crisis?

Thursday Psalm 121
How does God help your family during painful circumstances?

Friday Jeremiah 29:11
How can the promise of this passage encourage your family?

Saturday Romans 8:28
How could believing this Scripture affect your outlook on family problems?

⋯⋯⋯⋯ (fold here) ⋯⋯⋯⋯

TABLE™ TENT

"The Lord is my Shepherd . . ."
(Psalm 23:1).

KNOCK! KNOCK! KNOCK!

z-z-z-z

Having only one bathroom was a daily crisis for the Smurkelson family.

⋯⋯⋯⋯ (fold here) ⋯⋯⋯⋯

TABLE™ TENT

TALK TRIGGERS

◆ Who's the first person you turn to when you feel hurt? Why?

◆ Why do you think God allows families to go through tough times?

Struggles Kids Face, Week 3
Permission to photocopy this handout granted for local church use.
Copyright © Group Publishing, Inc., Box 481, Loveland, CO 80539.

WHAT DID YOU SAY?

THE POINT

☞ **What we say reflects who we are.**

THE BIBLE BASIS

Psalm 34:11-14

> Children, come and listen to me. I will teach you to worship the Lord. You must do these things to enjoy life and have many happy days. You must not say evil things, and you must not tell lies. Stop doing evil and do good. Look for peace and work for it.

"Children, come and listen to me," says King David in **Psalm 34:11.** It evokes the image of a man about to give away a secret. He goes on: "I will teach you to worship the Lord... to enjoy life and to have many happy days. You must not say evil things..." For David, an important key to worship, enjoyment, and happy days is simply learning how to control what you say.

Learning how to manage their mouths can be a monumental task for fifth- and sixth-graders. Many kids pick up swearing and profanity from their peers at school. Even the nicest kids can be tempted to experiment with bad language because it makes them feel "grown-up." Like adults, kids sometimes view bad language as a normal outlet for anger. Still others use profanity or unkind words simply to gain attention. Kids need to realize that part of making Jesus master of their lives means making him master of their mouths.

Use this lesson to let kids in on King David's secret and to challenge them to follow God's standards for speech. Other Scriptures used in the lesson are **Matthew 12:33-37; James 3:2-10;** and **Ephesians 4:29-31.**

GETTING THE POINT

Students will
◆ discuss the temptation to use bad language,
◆ examine how words reflect a person's heart, and
◆ practice saying encouraging words.

THIS LESSON AT A GLANCE

SECTION	MINUTES	WHAT STUDENTS WILL DO	LEARNING LAB SUPPLIES	CLASSROOM SUPPLIES
ATTENTION GRABBER	5 to 10	**Sooty Definitions**—Compare bad language to a soot stick.	Soot stick	
BIBLE EXPLORATION AND APPLICATION	9 to 14	**Goo-Goo Head**—Talk about what tempts them to use bad language, then examine Psalm 34:11-14.		Bibles, newsprint, marker, doughnuts
	8 to 13	**I Hear You**—Listen to people saying both positive and negative things and discuss Matthew 12:33-37 and James 3:2-10.	Cassette: "I Hear You"	Bibles, cassette player
	8 to 13	**Practice Makes Perfect**—Practice saying encouraging words and talk about Ephesians 4:29-31.	Learning Lab lid, flippers	Bibles, masking tape
CLOSING	5 to 10	**As Good as God's Word**—Sing a song as a reminder to make their words communicate God's Word.	Cassette: "Thy Word," lyrics poster	Cassette player
MODULE REVIEW	up to 5	**Reflection**—Review what they've learned over the past four lessons.		

Remember to make photocopies of the "Table Tent" handout (p. 54) to send home with your kids. The "Table Tent" is a valuable tool for helping fifth- and sixth-graders talk with their parents about what they're learning in class.

THE LESSON

Before the lesson, collect the necessary items from the Learning Lab for the activities you plan to use. Refer to the pictures in the margins to see what each item looks like.

As kids arrive, ask them about last week's "Table Tent" discussion. Use questions such as "What did you learn about your family?" and "What surprised you about your family's reactions?" However, be careful not to embarrass students whose families choose not to use the "Table Tent."

ATTENTION GRABBER

SOOTY DEFINITIONS

(5 to 10 minutes)

Begin class with a reminder to kids that whenever you sound the *squeaker*, they're to stop what they're doing, raise their hands, and focus on you. Practice the signal two or three times.

Form a circle and say: **Today we're going to talk about bad language, but before we do that we need to define what bad language is.**

Pass the *soot stick* around the circle and have kids take turns telling how they'd define "bad language." Have kids rub the *soot stick* between their palms while they give their definitions. Kids might say things like "Bad language is putting others down" or "Bad language is using profanity."

Afterward, retrieve the *soot stick* for later use. Have kids look at their soot-covered hands. Ask:

◆ **How would you describe your hands right now?** (Sooty; dirty; messy; disgusting.)

◆ **How is the way the *soot stick* affected your hands like the way bad language affects our lives?** (Bad language "dirties" our life; bad language makes you look and feel bad.)

Say: ✍ **Because what we say reflects who we are, it's important for us to know how to manage our mouths. Let's talk more about what this means.**

LEARNING LAB

TEACHER TIP

It's important to say The Point just as it's written in each activity. Repeating The Point over and over throughout the lesson will help kids remember it and apply it to their lives.

✎ THE **POINT**

BIBLE EXPLORATION AND APPLICATION

GOO-GOO HEAD

(9 to 14 minutes)

Say: **I hate it when people put me down and call me a "goo-goo head," but I get called that anyway. I'd like to take a survey to find out why. As I read each of the following questions from my survey, stand on my left if you'd answer "yes" or stand on my right if you'd answer "no." Then I'll see if I can find out why people insist on calling me a goo-goo head.**

Read the questions from the "Goo-Goo Head Survey" and see how kids respond.

Afterward, form groups of no more than three and say: **Well, I don't want you to call me a goo-goo head, but I've got doughnuts for you anyway. You can eat them as we discuss the following questions.**

Pass out the doughnuts for kids to enjoy and have trios discuss the following questions. Write the questions on newsprint for groups to refer to during discussions. Ask:

◆ **What's your reaction to what you just did?** (It was fun; I was surprised how easy it was to answer "yes"; I was disappointed because no one cared that you hate being called a goo-goo head.)

◆ **What tempted you to answer "yes" to the survey questions?** (Everyone else was answering "yes"; I wouldn't like it if you called me a goo-goo head first; I wanted the doughnut reward.)

◆ **What tempts you to include bad language like put-downs in the way you talk in real life?** (All my friends use profanity; others call me names; it makes you feel like you're better than others if you put them down.)

◆ **What did you discover about your attitude toward put-downs from your responses to the goo-goo head survey?** (I don't worry too much about put-downs; it's tempting to use put-downs, especially if they're funny.)

Sound the *squeaker* to end the small-group discussions. Wait for everyone to respond by raising their hands and focusing on you. Have the oldest person in each trio share his or her group's answers to the first question, the next oldest share answers to the second question, and so on.

Next, have the person wearing the most buttons in each trio read **Psalm 34:11-14** aloud for his or her group. Have the other trio members summarize the passage in one sentence. Then ask:

◆ **How would your answers during the "Goo-Goo Head Survey" have been different if I'd read Psalm 34:11-14 first? Explain?** (I'd have said "no" to more of the questions because I'd remember God doesn't want me to say mean things; I still might've said "yes" because I'd only be joking.)

◆ **What would life be like if everyone you knew lived by the standards set in Psalm 34:11-14?** (People would be easier to talk to; people would be less likely to argue or fight; we'd all be closer to God.)

◆ **What makes it hard for you to control what you say?** (Everybody else uses bad language around me, so it just slips out; it's a habit; my friends and I always put each other down.)

◆ **What can you do this week to overcome the temptation to use profanity and put-downs?** (I can read **Psalm 34:11-14;** I can ask God to help me pay attention to my words; I can make an agreement with my friends to stop using bad language.)

Say: **It's easy to give in to the temptation to use bad language. But, because ✍ what we say reflects who we are, we need to do as Psalm 34:11-14 advises and be careful with our words.**

✍ THE **POINT**

I HEAR YOU 📖

LEARNING LAB

(8 to 13 minutes)

Form a circle and say: **Listen to this tape segment of people talking. Think about how you'd feel if these people were talking to you.**

Play "I Hear You" from the *cassette.*

Afterward, have each student pair up with the person across from him or her in the circle. Have partners discuss these questions one at a time and take turns reporting their answers after each discussion. Ask:

◆ **How did listening to these people talking make you feel? Explain.** (I was mad at that first girl because she was so mean; I felt sorry for the guy who said he was a moron; it felt good to hear the positive people.)

◆ **How does what you heard on the tape compare to real-life conversations?** (Kids make fun of other kids at school all the time; I have a really encouraging teacher in one of my classes; I've sometimes told myself I was dumb.)

◆ **Based on what they said, what are your impressions of the people on this tape?** (The coach is mean; the teacher is kind and cares about her kids; the guy who said he was a moron doesn't think much of himself.)

Have kids answer this question silently instead of talking about it with their partners: **Which person on the *cassette* sounded most like you? Why?**

Give kids 30 seconds or so to think about the last question. Then have partners take turns reading and summarizing **Matthew 12:33-37** and **James 3:2-10.** Afterward, ask:

◆ **Why do you think God is concerned about the way we talk to others?** (Because God knows our words reflect our hearts; because God wants us to help each other with our words, not hurt each other.)

◆ **How can controlling what we say affect who we are?** (It can help us think positive thoughts before we speak; it can make us friendlier people; it can show others how God is working in our hearts.)

◆ **What can we do this week to encourage each other to speak positively instead of negatively?** (Practice saying kind things to others; pray for each other.)

THE **POINT**

Say: Because what we say reflects who we are, we need to make sure our speech reflects God's love.

Lead kids in a prayer similar to this: **Lord, before we go any further, we'd like to ask for your help in controlling the way we talk. Help our words this week show others the good things you've created inside us. In Jesus' name, amen.**

LEARNING LAB

PRACTICE MAKES PERFECT

(8 to 13 minutes)

Clear an open area in the middle of the room and use masking tape to mark a 5-foot circle on the floor. Place the Learning Lab lid upside down in the center of the circle and have kids sit around the outside of the circle. Give each student one of the *flippers.*

Say: **The object of this game is to see how many *flippers* we can flip from the edge of the circle into the box. We'll have 30 seconds to practice, then we'll all flip our *flippers* at the same time for the real thing. Start practicing now.**

Sound the *squeaker* after 30 seconds to end the practice time. After everyone has responded by raising their hands and focusing on you, have kids flip their *flippers* all at once toward the lid.

Collect any *flippers* that didn't make it into the Learning Lab lid. Congratulate everyone for their efforts and ask:

◆ **How did practicing affect your success at this game?** (Practicing showed me exactly how to flip the *flipper;* practicing helped me get my aim down; I was better after practice.)

Say: **Just as it took practice to be able to flip a *flipper* into the box, it takes practice to learn how to speak to others in an encouraging way. Let's practice that right now.**

Count the number of *flippers* that made it into the Learning Lab lid and have kids think of the same number of things they like about the person sitting on their left. Put away the Learning Lab items while kids take a moment to think. Then have kids take turns sharing what they like about the people they're sitting next to.

For example, if there are three *flippers* in the Learning Lab lid, a student might say, "Three things I like about Rhonda are she's always friendly, she's a good listener, and she's fun to be around."

Have kids raise their hands as you ask the following questions. When one student shares an answer, have anyone who thought of the same answer and has nothing more to add lower his or her hand. When all hands are down, ask the next question and repeat the process.

◆ **How did you feel as we practiced encouraging each other? Explain.** (Good, it was neat to hear people say what they liked about me; like I wanted to tell more things I liked about the person on my left; unsure, because I'm not used to doing things like that.)

◆ **How does this encouragement activity compare to real life?** (We're more likely to tell others what we don't like about them than what we do like; it always feels good when others say encouraging things to me.)

◆ **Why do you think we need to practice saying encouraging things?** (Because we don't do it often enough; because no matter how good we are at it, we can always get better.)

Have everyone read **Ephesians 4:29-31** in unison. Then ask:

◆ **How was Ephesians 4:29-31 reflected in our encouragement activity?** (We said kind things to each other instead of hurtful things; the things we shared can encourage others to grow stronger in the qualities we talked about.)

◆ **What do you suppose God thought about the way we practiced encouraging each other? Explain.** (I think God liked it because it made us practice following **Ephesians 4:29-31;** I think God might've been disappointed because we

TEACHER TIP

If you have more than 20 students in class, have kids form pairs and take turns flipping their *flippers.* If you have less than 10 students, you may want to give each person two *flippers.*

If no one is able to make a *flipper* flip into the box, have kids move six to 12 inches closer to the Learning Lab lid and try again. Allow kids to keep trying until at least one *flipper* makes it in.

TEACHER TIP

In some classes, students don't know each other well enough to think of several things they like about each other. If that's the case with your kids, have the entire class think of things they like about each person instead.

THE POINT ✍

didn't try too hard at our practice.)

Say: **We are God's children, so let's be sure that** ✍ **what we say reflects who we are. Remember that as you practice saying encouraging things all week long.**

TABLE™
TENT

We believe Christian education extends beyond the classroom into the home. Photocopy the "Table Tent" handout (p. 54) for this week and send it home with your kids. Encourage kids and parents to use the handout to spark meaningful discussion on this week's topic. Follow up next week by asking kids how their discussions went with their families.

CLOSING

LEARNING LAB

THE POINT ✍

AS GOOD AS GOD'S WORD

(5 to 10 minutes)

Show kids the words to the song "Thy Word," printed on the *lyrics poster*. Ask:

◆ **What can we learn about God's Word from this song?** (God's Word guides us; God's Word can help calm our fears; God's Word tells us of God's love.)

Say: **Just as** ✍ **what we say reflects who we are, God's Word reflects who God is. Through the Bible we can hear God's words of love, guidance, and encouragement for us. Let's sing "Thy Word" as a reminder to let God's Word guide the way we communicate with others.**

Lead kids in singing "Thy Word." Use the *cassette tape* and the *lyrics poster* to assist you.

MODULE REVIEW

REFLECTION

(up to 5 minutes)

Form a circle and say: **Think for a moment about what you've learned today and during the previous three class sessions. Be ready to share your thoughts.**

Before dismissing class, have kids go around the circle and take turns completing one of these sentences:

◆ "One important thing I've learned today is…"

◆ "An important thing I've learned from one of the previous three class sessions is…"

◆ "If I told my friends about this class, I'd say…"

Martin always got in trouble for his "fowl" language.

TABLE™ TENT

"You must not say evil things, and you must not tell lies"
(Psalm 34:13).

Talk Triggers

▲ Based on what you say, what would a stranger think about you?

▲ When are you most tempted to use put-downs or bad language? What can you do about it?

THE WORD on Bad Language

Monday   Exodus 20:7
How do people misuse the Lord's name? How would you feel if people used your name like that? Explain.

Tuesday   James 5:12
What does it take for people to believe what you say? Why?

Wednesday   Ephesians 4:15
How does a person "speak the truth with love"?

Thursday   1 Timothy 4:12
What kind of example do you set with your words?

Friday   2 Timothy 2:16
What makes it hard for you to follow the instructions of this passage? What can you do about it?

Saturday   2 Timothy 4:2
How can God use the things you say to help others know Jesus better?

NEW LIFE IN CHRIST

BY
JANE VOGEL AND PAUL WOODS

Ahh, spring! Flowers are blooming, grass is growing, and birds have come home for the summer. As **Song of Solomon 2:11-12a** describes it, "Look, the winter is past; the rains are over and gone. Blossoms appear through all the land." After the cold, drab days of winter, the world comes back to life before our very eyes.

Everyone gets caught up in the hope and joy of spring, including your fifth- and sixth-graders. What better time to reintroduce your students to Jesus—the giver of life—who died and came back to life himself? Many of your fifth- and sixth-graders may need more than a *re*introduction; some have never met Jesus or experienced his life-giving power at all.

Research indicates that among fifth- and sixth-graders *who regularly attend church,* roughly one in four doesn't know who Jesus is. Two out of every five don't know why Jesus had to die. And, approximately one-third don't know that Jesus came back to life after his death and burial.

Each spring day, kids are spotting signs of new life in the world around them. Make sure they're not missing out on the new life found in Jesus. Use these five lessons to introduce your students to new life, Jesus-style!

——— FIVE LESSONS ON NEW LIFE IN CHRIST ———

LEARNING LAB

THE SIGNAL ▬▬▬▬▬▬▬

During the lessons on New Life in Christ, your signal to get kids' attention will be to squeeze the *squeaker* found in the Learning Lab. In response to the *squeaker*, have kids immediately stop what they're doing, raise their hands, and focus on you.

Tell kids about this signal—and practice it—before the lesson begins. Explain that it's important to respond to this signal quickly so the class can do as many fun activities as possible. During the lessons, you'll be prompted when to use the signal.

LEARNING LAB

THE TIME STUFFER ▬▬▬▬▬

This module's Time Stuffer will encourage kids to describe what they're learning about new life in Christ. Hang the *Tell Me About It!* poster found in the Learning Lab in a prominent place in the room. You'll need scissors, a stack of old magazines, and push pins nearby.

When kids have a few moments during or after the lesson, they can cut out words or phrases from the magazines that describe how they would complete the sentences on the poster. For example, an ad that reads "Just Do It" might reflect a student's anticipation of Jesus' return. Or an article that has "Wow!" in the title might reflect someone's feelings about Jesus' power over life and death.

Encourage kids to be creative in choosing and arranging the words they cut out. Periodically over the next five weeks, remove old phrases from the poster to make room for new ones.

RESURRECTION POWER

THE POINT

☞ **God has power over life and death.**

THE BIBLE BASIS

Romans 8:10-13

> Your body will always be dead because of sin. But if Christ is in you, then the Spirit gives you life, because Christ made you right with God. God raised Jesus from the dead, and if God's Spirit is living in you, he will also give life to your bodies that die. God is the One who raised Christ from the dead, and he will give life through his Spirit that lives in you.
>
> So, my brothers and sisters, we must not be ruled by our sinful selves or live the way our sinful selves want. If you use your lives to do the wrong things your sinful selves want, you will die spiritually. But if you use the Spirit's help to stop doing the wrong things you do with your body, you will have true life.

Nowhere is the power of God more awesomely displayed than in Jesus' resurrection. This miracle that could be seen and touched by hundreds of people changed the course of history forever. And God has promised to use that same miraculous, life-giving power to free us from the deadly influence of sin.

Fifth- and sixth-graders may have a hard time understanding the concept of being dead in sin. But they know what it is to die a little every time they suffer a put-down at school, hear their parents fighting, or fail at something important to them.

In this lesson, fifth- and sixth-graders will learn that the same power that raised Jesus from the dead is available today to those who trust God.

Another Scripture used in the lesson is **Matthew 28:1-20.**

GETTING THE POINT

Students will
◆ learn that God did the impossible by raising Jesus from the dead,
◆ discover that only God can give life, and
◆ discuss how Jesus' resurrection power can help them live for God.

THIS LESSON AT A GLANCE

SECTION	MINUTES	WHAT STUDENTS WILL DO	LEARNING LAB SUPPLIES	CLASSROOM SUPPLIES
ATTENTION GRABBER	5 to 10	**Confetti Votes**—Vote for the top three situations that make them feel powerless.	Plastic confetti	Paper, pen, masking tape, newsprint, marker
BIBLE EXPLORATION AND APPLICATION	10 to 15	**The Day the Impossible Happened**—Balance stones on their foreheads while doing jumping jacks, then explore the story of Jesus' resurrection in Matthew 28:1-20.	Scented stones, squeaker, cassette: "The Day the Impossible Happened"	Bibles, cassette player
	8 to 13	**Flight Simulations**—Discover implications of Romans 8:10-11 after competing to fly a butterfly.	Feather butterfly	Bibles
	7 to 12	**Tree-Chain Saw-Rain**—Play a variation of the Rock-Paper-Scissors game and discuss Romans 8:10-13.	Squeaker	Bibles
CLOSING	5 to 10	**Knights of the Kingdom**—Affirm God's power in each other.	Inflatable sword	

Remember to make photocopies of the "Table Tent" handout (p. 66) to send home with your kids. The "Table Tent" is a valuable tool for helping fifth- and sixth-graders talk with their parents about what they're learning in class.

THE LESSON

Before the lesson, collect the necessary items from the Learning Lab for the activities you plan to use. Refer to the pictures in the margins to see what each item looks like.

As kids arrive, ask them about last week's "Table Tent" discussion. Use questions such as "What did you learn about your family?" and "What surprised you about your family's reactions?" However, be careful not to embarrass students whose families choose not to use the "Table Tent."

ATTENTION GRABBER

CONFETTI VOTES

(5 to 10 minutes)

Begin class with a reminder to kids that whenever you sound the *squeaker*, they're to stop what they're doing, raise their hands, and focus on you. Practice the signal two or three times.

Have kids brainstorm a list of 10 different real-life situations that would make them or other fifth- and sixth-graders feel powerless. For example, kids might say parents getting a divorce, moving to a new school, being sick, being bullied, failing school, a death in the family, family financial problems, and so on.

Write the items from your list on separate sheets of paper, then use masking tape to post the sheets at different places around the room. Next, give every student a handful of the *plastic confetti*.

Say: **Take a minute to think about which three of these 10 situations you would feel the most powerless in.** (Pause.)

Now, vote for your top three choices by distributing your *plastic confetti* in piles beneath the signs. Place the most confetti under your first choice, a smaller amount under your second choice, and the smallest amount under your third choice. It's all right if your piles mix together with other people's piles under the signs. Go.

Give kids one minute to vote. Then sound the *squeaker* to call time. After everyone has responded by raising their hands and focusing on you, see which situation's sign has the most confetti under it.

Next, have kids give the "thumbs up" sign as you ask the following questions. When one student shares an answer, kids

LEARNING LAB

TEACHER TIP

If you feel it's necessary, let kids know that wisecracks and put-downs aren't acceptable during brainstorming.

Also, it's helpful to write kids' ideas on newsprint as the group brainstorms its list.

who thought of the same answer and have nothing more to add can drop their hands. When all thumbs are down, ask the next question and repeat the process. Ask:

◆ **What were you thinking when you voted?** (That I'm glad none of these things has happened to me; how it was hard to pick only three; that we all voted for the same things.)

◆ **Why do you think** (the situation that has the most confetti under it) **has the largest pile?** (Because it's the worst one; a lot of people have to deal with that.)

◆ **Why do we feel powerless in these kinds of situations?** (Because we don't know what to do; because we can't control what happens.)

Say: **Two thousand years ago, Jesus' followers were in a situation that made them feel powerless and afraid. The Jewish leaders and Roman authorities had killed Jesus. But** ☞ **God has power over life and death, and on the third day Jesus came back to life. He lives today and will continue to live forever.**

That same power that raised Jesus from the dead is available to us today. Let's learn more about Jesus' resurrection power now.

TEACHER TIP

It's important to say The Point just as it's written in each activity. Repeating The Point over and over throughout the lesson will help kids remember it and apply it to their lives.

THE **POINT** ☞

BIBLE EXPLORATION AND APPLICATION

LEARNING

TEACHER TIP

If you have more students than *scented stones*, form pairs (or trios) and have partners take turns using the *scented stones* for the activity.

THE DAY THE IMPOSSIBLE HAPPENED

(10 to 15 minutes)

Give everyone one of the *scented stones*.

Say: **Look toward the ceiling and balance your *scented stone* on your forehead.** (Pause)

When I sound the *squeaker*, do jumping jacks until I sound the *squeaker* again. If your stone falls, stop jumping. Be careful not to step on or break any *scented stones* that fall on the floor.

Sound the *squeaker* to begin the jumping jacks. Make sure kids are really jumping—not just moving their arms. Don't give the signal until everyone's *scented stone* has fallen off. (It won't take long!)

Afterward, say: **Well, maybe that was too difficult. Let's try something else.**

Have kids balance their *scented stones* on their foreheads again and jog briskly around the room. Tell kids to keep jogging until you sound the *squeaker*. Again, don't sound the *squeaker* until everyone's stone has fallen.

Then collect the *scented stones* for use in later lessons and form groups of four. Direct students to number off within their groups from one to four.

Say: **Discuss the next few questions in your groups. Then I'll call out a number from one to four. The person in your group whose number I call will be responsible for sharing your answer.**

Ask:

◆ **How did it feel to try to keep the *scented stone* on your forehead? Explain.** (Frustrating, because it was impossible; like I should just give up.)

◆ **What things are impossible for you in real life?** (I can't fly; I can't get straight A's; I can't make the sun stop shining.)

Say: **Although some things are impossible for us, nothing is impossible for God. Let's hear about a day when God did the impossible.**

Play "The Day the Impossible Happened," a dramatic reading of **Matthew 28:1-20,** from the *cassette.*

Afterward, have foursomes discuss these questions:

◆ **How does the way you felt during the balancing activity compare to how Jesus' followers might've felt during this story?** (They were probably confused like we were; they probably felt like Jesus' coming back to life was impossible.)

◆ **Why do you think God did this impossible thing of raising Jesus from the dead?** (To show God's power; to make it possible for us to know God; to defeat the devil once and for all.)

◆ **If you had lived at that time, would you have believed that Jesus came back to life? Why or why not?** (Yes, because lots of people saw him; no, it would've seemed impossible.)

◆ **What helps you believe that Jesus rose from the dead?** (The disciples all saw Jesus; too many people are Christians for it to be a hoax; I know Jesus is alive because he lives in my heart.)

◆ **How does it make you feel to know that Jesus has the power to defeat death? Explain.** (Amazed, because that's more power than I can understand; great, because he's on my side; unsure, because I'm not sure I can believe it.)

◆ **How has Jesus shown his power in your life?** (He's given me the ability to be patient with my sister; he's helped my dad find a job.)

Say: **Nothing was impossible for God in Jesus' time, and nothing is impossible for God today.** 🖝 **God has power over life and death. So, let Jesus' resurrection encourage you this week when you face "impossible" situations.**

LEARNING LAB

FLIGHT SIMULATIONS 📖

(8 to 13 minutes)

Form pairs. Hold up the *feather butterfly* and say: **You and your partner will have one opportunity to make this butterfly "fly" in the most lifelike way possible.**

I'll be judging your attempts on a scale of 1 to 10, based on distance covered, how long it stays in the air without being touched by either partner, and whether or not it stays right-side-up. You may take one minute now to plan your strategy. Go.

After about a minute, sound the *squeaker* to regain kids' attention. When everyone responds by raising their hands and focusing on you, give the *feather butterfly* to the first pair. Let them "fly" it however they wish—throwing it, blowing it, or whatever.

Afterward, applaud the pair's effort and call out a score. Then pass the *feather butterfly* to the next pair and repeat the process. After every pair has had a turn, retrieve the *feather butterfly* for use in later lessons.

Have partners discuss the following questions one at a time, taking turns reporting their answers to the class after each discussion. Ask:

◆ **What would you have needed to make the *feather butterfly* really look alive?** (A fishing line or something to suspend it in air; a special effects studio; a way to make its wings flap; it could never really look alive.)

◆ **What's the most lifelike nonliving thing you've ever seen?** (Monsters done with special effects in movies; stuffed animals in a museum; paintings or sculptures.)

Say: **Even with amazing special effects, we can only make things *look* lifelike. God, on the other hand, has the power to make things *alive*.**

Have one partner in each pair read **Romans 8:10-11** and the other summarize it in one sentence. Then ask:

◆ **In what ways can sin make us lifeless, like a *feather butterfly*?** (Sin can take away the joy of living; sin can separate us from God, who gives life.)

◆ **How did our efforts to give life to the *feather butterfly* compare to God's power to give life?** (Our butterfly

TEACHER TIP

When an activity calls for pairs, you can serve as one of the partners if your class has an uneven number of kids.

To avoid embarrassing anyone, you may want to make it a policy to rate each pair's attempt a five or above.

never came to life; only God can really make something alive.)

◆ **What kind of life does Jesus promise for those who believe in him?** (Life in heaven after we die; life with him here on earth; life free from the power of sin.)

◆ **This week, how can God's life-giving power work in you?** (I can ask Jesus to live in me; through prayer; through reading the Bible; by remembering Romans 8:10-11.)

Say: **Jesus' resurrection is proof that ✍ God has power over life and death. Romans 8:10-11 makes it clear that God is willing to use that power to give *us* life as well. Let's take a few moments right now to silently thank God for that gift of life.**

Have the class spend 30 to 60 seconds in silence before going on to the next activity. You may want to invite kids to talk with you after class about receiving God's gift of life.

✎ THE **POINT**

TREE-CHAIN SAW-RAIN

LEARNING LAB

(7 to 12 minutes)

If you skipped the previous activity, have kids form pairs. Have partners face each other. Tell kids they're going to play Tree-Chain Saw-Rain, a game like Rock-Paper-Scissors, then teach the following motions. Have kids practice each motion as you teach it.

Tree—Hold hands over head like branches and say, "Rustle, rustle, rustle."

Chain Saw—Pretend to hold a chain saw and buzz noisily.

Rain—Wiggle fingers through the air and say, "Pitter-patter, pitter-patter."

Say: **The chain saw overpowers the tree because it can cut the tree down. The rain overpowers the chain saw because it causes rust. The tree overpowers rain because it drinks up rain. If what you do overpowers what your partner does, you get 1 point.**

Have kids stand back-to-back and take three seconds to decide which motion they're going to do. When you sound the *squeaker,* have kids turn around and choose tree, chain saw, or rain. Tell kids to keep track of their own points. Play three or four rounds.

Afterward, just for fun, see which class member scored the most points. Then ask:

◆ **How did you feel during this game? Explain.** (Good, because I got a lot of points; worried, because no matter what I chose, there was always something that could overpower it.)

◆ **What made it hard to choose a position of power?** (I never knew what my partner was going to do; there was always a chance that she would choose the position that could overpower mine; no position was all-powerful.)

◆ **How was this game like life?** (They're both unpredictable; there's always somebody or something stronger than you are.)

Next, have one partner in each pair read **Romans 8:10-11** and the other read **Romans 8:12-13.** Then ask:

◆ **How does Jesus' ability to conquer death compare to our ability to win this game?** (Jesus' resurrection power gives more than points; nothing can beat Jesus' resurrection power.)

◆ **What kind of power does sin have in our lives?** (Sin leads us away from God; no matter how hard we try, we can't seem to stop doing wrong.)

◆ **When are you tempted to give in to sin and do wrong?** (When all my friends think it's OK; when I want something really badly; when I'm angry or depressed.)

◆ **How can Jesus' resurrection power give you power to defeat sin this week?** (By helping me recognize that I can depend on God; by helping me be strong enough to resist temptation.)

Say: **Sometimes it seems like sin is too powerful for us, but we need to remember that** 👉 **God has power over life and death. That same power that raised Jesus from the dead can help us follow the advice of Romans 8:10-13 this week and every week.**

THE **POINT** 👉

Have kids assume the appropriate positions as you pray this prayer: **God, give us life to grow strong like trees.** (Pause) **Give us your Holy Spirit to wash us clean like rain washes the ground.** (Pause) **Give us your resurrection power to cut down all the selfishness and temptations in our lives like a chain saw cuts wood.** (Pause) **In Jesus' name, amen.**

TABLE™ TENT

We believe Christian education extends beyond the classroom into the home. Photocopy the "Table Tent" handout (p. 66) for this week and send it home with your kids. Encourage kids and parents to use the handout to spark meaningful discussion on this week's topic. Follow up next week by asking kids how their discussions went with their families.

CLOSING

KNIGHTS OF THE KINGDOM

(5 to 10 minutes)

Take out the *inflatable sword* and blow it up.

Say: **In some countries, a person who has done something remarkable is knighted.**

Demonstrate by tapping a person lightly on each shoulder with the *inflatable sword.*

Say: **Because ✍ God has power over life and death, God did something remarkable by raising Jesus from the dead. Instead of keeping that power to himself, God is sharing it with us. Let's take a moment to recognize the small ways God's resurrection power can be seen in us.**

Ask kids to each think of a way to complete this sentence for the person on their right: "I see God's resurrection power in your..." Kids might fill in the blank by saying things like, "in your commitment to God," "in your reaching out to others," or "in your smile."

After a moment of "think-time," start the knighting process by tapping the person to your right on both shoulders with the *inflatable sword* as you complete the sentence. Pass the sword around the circle until everyone has been affirmed.

Before dismissing class, have kids tell a partner their answers to the following question: **What will you do differently next week because of this lesson?** (I'll thank Jesus for sharing his resurrection power with me; I'll tell a friend about how Jesus gives life; I'll ask God to help me in impossible situations.)

LEARNING LAB

☞ THE **POINT**

TABLE™
TENT

"God is the One who raised Christ from the dead, and he will give life through his Spirit that lives in you" (Romans 8:11b).

Talk Triggers

◆ How have you seen God's power at work in your life? in the lives of others?

◆ In what area of your life do you need God's power the most? Explain.

THE WORD on Resurrection Power

Monday   Isaiah 53:8-11
How was this prophecy fulfilled in Jesus' death and resurrection? How can it be fulfilled in your life?

Tuesday   Acts 2:22-28
How would you have responded if you'd been in the crowd that heard Peter's sermon? Explain.

Wednesday   1 Corinthians 15:12-20
Why do you think Paul places such importance on the truth of Jesus' resurrection?

Thursday   Ephesians 2:4-10
In what ways can Jesus' resurrection affect your life?

Friday   Romans 8:31-39
How does reading this passage make you feel about your relationship with God?

Saturday   1 Corinthians 15:51-58
How is the promise of this passage validated by Jesus' resurrection?

(fold here)

When angels first discovered Jesus' empty tomb.

YES!

New Life in Christ, Week 5

NEW AND IMPROVED

THE POINT

☞ **Only God makes us new.**

THE BIBLE BASIS

2 Corinthians 5:17

> If anyone belongs to Christ, there is a new creation. The old things have gone; everything is made new!

A temper tuck here, a nosiness job there... Fixing those little flaws in our personalities—who wouldn't welcome a chance at a divine makeover? But **2 Corinthians 5:17** makes it clear that we need more than just a makeover. The old has to go—completely. We don't need to be refurbished; we need to be made new. And only God can do it.

Fifth- and sixth-graders are a complex of contradictory emotions. They want independence, yet they feel inadequate. They're proud of the way they're maturing, yet they feel insecure about who they'll become. They're constantly trying new things to be smarter, prettier, more popular, more athletic, and so on. Kids need to know that our human attempts at self-improvement are feeble at best—only God can make us new.

Other Scriptures used in this lesson are **1 John 1:8-9; Romans 3:23-24; Hebrews 10:17; Psalm 32:5;** and **Isaiah 1:18.**

GETTING THE POINT

Students will
- ◆ discover why they need God to make them new creations,
- ◆ compare craft makeovers to God's new creations, and
- ◆ examine the renewing power of God's forgiveness.

THIS LESSON AT A GLANCE

SECTION	MINUTES	WHAT STUDENTS WILL DO	LEARNING LAB SUPPLIES	CLASSROOM SUPPLIES
ATTENTION GRABBER	5 to 10	**Ad-Venture**—Compete to find ads for new and improved products.		Old magazines, old newspapers
BIBLE EXPLORATION AND APPLICATION	8 to 13	**More Than a Makeover**—Give makeovers to newsprint faces and discuss 1 John 1:8-9 and 2 Corinthians 5:17.	Soot stick, scented stones, elastic strips, flippers, plastic confetti, mini straw hat	Bibles, newsprint, cellophane tape, pencils, paper
	10 to 15	**Missing the Mark**—Improve a game and examine Romans 3:23-24 and 2 Corinthians 5:17.	Flippers, carpenter wreath, mini straw hat	Bibles
	7 to 12	**The Unforgettable Sin**—Explore the meaning of Hebrews 10:17; Psalm 32:5; and Isaiah 1:18 after hearing a story about forgiveness.	Cassette: "The Unforgettable Sin"	Bibles, cassette player, pencils, paper, trash can
CLOSING	5 to 10	**New-You Awards**—Give awards recognizing God's creative, renewing work in each other.		Paper, pencils
Remember to make photocopies of the "Table Tent" handout (p. 76) to send home with your kids. The "Table Tent" is a valuable tool for helping fifth- and sixth-graders talk with their parents about what they're learning in class.				

THE LESSON

Before the lesson, collect the necessary items from the Learning Lab for the activities you plan to use. Refer to the pictures in the margins to see what each item looks like.

As kids arrive, ask them about last week's "Table Tent" discussion. Use questions such as "What did you learn about your family?" and "What surprised you about your family's reactions?" However, be careful not to embarrass students whose families choose not to use the "Table Tent."

ATTENTION GRABBER

AD-VENTURE

(5 to 10 minutes)

Begin class with a reminder that whenever you sound the *squeaker,* kids are to stop what they're doing, raise their hands, and focus on you. Practice the signal two or three times.

Form two teams. Give each team a stack of old magazines and newspapers.

Say: **You have three minutes to tear out as many ads, articles, or coupons as you can find that promote a "new" or "improved" product. Each item you tear out must say somewhere that it's new, improved, or somehow better that it was before. Ready? Go.**

After three minutes, call time with the *squeaker.* When everyone has responded by raising their hands and focusing on you, count up the number of ads, articles, and coupons each team tore out. Applaud both teams for their efforts.

Have kids choose a partner from the opposing team and discuss this question in their pairs: **What did you learn from what you just did?** (There are lots of products that claim to be new or improved; people want to buy new things.)

Sound the *squeaker* to pause discussions. After everyone responds by raising their hands and focusing on you, have pairs report their answers to the class. Repeat the process for each remaining question. Ask:

◆ **Why do you think people are attracted to new or improved things?** (Everyone thinks new is better; people want to have the best things; people get tired of the same old things.)

◆ **When do you feel "new and improved"?** (When I get new clothes; when I get a fun haircut; when I'm able to do something that was hard for me before.)

LEARNING LAB

TEACHER TIP

It's important to say The Point just as it's written in each activity. Repeating The Point over and over throughout the lesson will help kids remember it and apply it to their lives.

THE **POINT**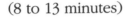

Say: **It's great to improve our looks or abilities, but** **only God makes us new inside and out. Today we're going to learn more about how and why God does that.**

BIBLE EXPLORATION AND APPLICATION

LEARNING LAB

MORE THAN A MAKEOVER

(8 to 13 minutes)

Use the *soot stick* to draw the outline of a large head on each of four sheets of newsprint. Leave the faces blank (no facial features) and hairless.

Form four groups (a group can be one person) and give each group one of the sheets of newsprint. Place the *soot stick, scented stones, flippers, elastic strips, plastic confetti, mini straw hat,* and cellophane tape in a central location.

Say: **As you can see, the face on your newsprint needs a little help.** (Point to the Learning Lab supplies.) **In just a minute, your group will get to use these supplies to give your newsprint face a "makeover."**

For example, you may lay your face on the floor and sprinkle *plastic confetti* to make colorful hair. Or you could use the *scented stones* to make eyes and the *flippers* to make eyebrows and a mustache. Or you might make a bow tie out of the *elastic strips*. You can do anything as long as it isn't permanent, so be creative. Take a minute now to brainstorm ideas for your makeover, then go ahead and create a new face.

Give kids three to five minutes to complete their work. Afterward, allow kids to walk around and view each other's makeovers. Next, have kids choose partners from each of the other groups to form discussion groups of no more than four.

Have each group appoint one person to record their responses to the questions, one person to read **1 John 1:8-9** and **2 Corinthians 5:17,** one person to report their conclusions to the class, and one person to encourage everyone to participate in the discussion. Give paper and pencils to the recorders in each group and have the readers read the Scriptures. Then ask:

◆ **What did you like or dislike about this experience?** (I liked the creative way we used our supplies; it was fun to see what the other groups did; it was hard to think of what to make our face look like.)

◆ **In what ways do people "make over" their personalities or appearances in real life?** (They buy new clothes; they copy other·people's actions; they change their image.)

◆ **Why do people want to be made over?** (They're not happy with themselves; they realize they're not perfect; they want others to like them more.)

◆ **How do makeovers in personality or appearance compare to being made new as it's described in 1 John 1:8-9 and 2 Corinthians 5:17?** (Those makeovers are only surface deep, but God makes us new on the inside; those makeovers might not last, but God's work lasts forever.)

◆ **What keeps people from being made new by God?** (They don't ask God to make them new; they don't know God can make them new; they don't trust God to make them new.)

◆ **How can you allow God's power to make you new this week?** (I can ask God to make me new; I can look for ways God can work in my life; I can ask God to forgive me.)

◆ **How can you help others to allow God's power to make them new this week?** (I can tell them about God's promises in **2 Corinthians 5:17** and **1 John 1:8-9**; I can look for ways to encourage them.)

Sound the *squeaker* to regain everyone's attention. After kids respond by raising their hands and focusing on you, invite reporters from each group to share their conclusions with the class.

Say: **It's fun sometimes to make over our appearances or personalities, but  only God makes us new. Let's remember to call on and encourage God's renewing power in our lives this week.**

Enlist everyone's help to take apart and put away the Learning Lab items. Then say: **Now let's see what else we can learn about God's renewing power.**

MISSING THE MARK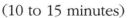

(10 to 15 minutes)

Form two new teams—team A and team B. Have each team form a single file line facing you. Place the *mini straw hat* on the floor in front of team A and the *carpenter wreath* on the floor in front of team B. Give the first person in each line five *flippers*.

☜ THE POINT

LEARNING LAB

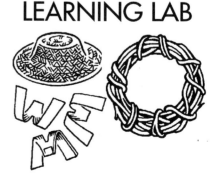

Say: **Each member of your team will have a turn to drop five *flippers* into the hat or inside the wreath. You must stand up straight—no stooping or bending—and hold your arm out straight at shoulder height when you drop the *flippers*. Your team will receive 100 points for every person who is able to make all five *flippers* land inside the hat or wreath.**

After everyone has had a turn, form two circles, one within the other. Have team A's members form the inner circle and face outward. Have team B's members form the outer circle and face inward.

Say: **The person facing you in the other circle is now your partner. Discuss my first question with him or her. Then rotate one position to the left for a new partner and answer my next question. Keep rotating and answering each new question with a new partner.**

After each question during this activity, give pairs time for discussion, then sound the *squeaker* to regain the group's attention. When everyone has responded by raising their hands and focusing on you, have pairs share their answers with the class.

Ask:

◆ **What did you think of this game?** (It was too hard; it was fun; it was frustrating.)

Have everyone in team A's circle read **Romans 3:23-24** aloud together. Then ask:

◆ **What did you learn in Romans 3:23-24 that applies to our game?** (Just like nobody is good enough for God's glory, nobody could win the game; we need help to succeed, just like we need help to follow God.)

◆ **What would you change about this game to make it better?** (I'd have us kneel while we drop the *flippers;* I'd have us get points for each *flipper* that lands in the wreath; I'd have somebody hold the hat.)

Pick two or three of the best ideas for changing the game and use them to make new rules. Then have teams play the game again. Afterward, collect the *mini straw hat, carpenter wreath,* and *flippers* for later use.

Re-form the two circles and have pairs discuss this question: **What did you think of this game after we made it better?** (It was still too hard; I liked it better the second time.)

Have everyone in team B's circle read **2 Corinthians 5:17** aloud together. Then ask:

◆ **How was the way we changed the game like or unlike the way God makes us new creations?** (We made the game better like God makes us better; we could never make the game as good as God can make us.)

◆ **Why do you think we need for God to make us new creations?** (Because we all fall short of God's standards; because we can't really change by ourselves.)

◆ **How does God make us new creations?** (By changing our hearts; by helping us become more like Jesus.)

◆ **How does the promise of 2 Corinthians 5:17 make you feel?** (Relieved to know that God can make the changes I want; unsure because I don't know if it's really true; excited that God cares enough to make me new.)

Say: **We can change the rules of a game, but**  **only God makes us new creations. It's exciting to think that God promises in 2 Corinthians 5:17 to do just that for you and me. Let's have a round of applause right now to express our thanks for God's creative work in us.**

Lead kids in a quick time of applause and cheers before moving on to the next activity.

 THE **POINT**

THE UNFORGETTABLE SIN

(7 to 12 minutes)

Gather kids in a circle and say: **The first step to being made new is simply trusting God to forgive the wrong things we've done. Let's listen to a story that talks abut that.**

Play "The Unforgettable Sin" from the *cassette*. Afterward, have volunteers read aloud **Hebrews 10:17; Psalm 32:5;** and **Isaiah 1:18.** Invite kids to summarize the themes of these passages.

Distribute paper and pencils to everyone. Then ask the following questions one at a time and have kids write their answers confidentially on their papers. Ask:

◆ **What surprised you about this story or these verses?** (That Jesus forgot the priest's sin; that God promises to forget our sins.)

◆ **When do you feel unforgivable, like the priest in this story?** (When I have a fight with my mom; when I do something I know is wrong; when I can't stop doing things that are wrong.)

◆ **Why do you think God promises to forgive and forget our wrongs if we ask him to?** (Because God loves us; because God wants to make us new; because God wants us to know him.)

◆ **How does experiencing God's forgiveness make us new?** (It gives us a fresh start; it relieves us of our guilty feelings; it helps us experience God's love.)

LEARNING LAB

TEACHER TIP

The story "The Unforgettable Sin" is taken from *Instant Devotions for Youth Ministry*, available from Group Publishing.

◆ **How can you experience the renewing power of God's forgiveness this week?** (By asking God to forgive me; by asking God to make me new; by trusting God to forgive the wrong I've done.)

◆ **How can you share the renewing power of God's forgiveness with others this week?** (Tell them the story of the priest; tell my friends about the Scriptures we read; forgive others when they do something I don't like.)

After everyone has had a chance to write an answer to each question, invite volunteers to share their answers with the class. Encourage sharing as long as time allows.

THE **POINT** ☞

Then say: ☞**Only God makes us new. God begins the renewing process by forgiving us when we ask him to. Think right now of the things for which you'd like God to forgive you. Using your finger as a pen with invisible ink, write those things on the bottom of your paper.**

Next, have everyone spend a moment in silent prayer, asking God to forgive the wrongs they've "written" on their papers.

After prayer, say: **When we ask God to forgive us, God also forgets the wrongs we've done. Since God has forgotten the things we've written down, let's forget them, too.**

Before moving on to the closing, have kids tear off the bottom of their papers. Then have kids rip those sections into little pieces and throw them into the trash.

TABLE™ TENT

We believe Christian education extends beyond the classroom into the home. Photocopy the "Table Tent" handout (p. 76) for this week and send it home with your kids. Encourage kids and parents to use the handout to spark meaningful discussion on this week's topic. Follow up next week by asking kids how their discussions went with their families.

CLOSING

NEW-YOU AWARDS

(5 to 10 minutes)

Give each student a blank sheet of paper and a pencil.

Say: **God's creative renewing work never stops. Let's take a minute to recognize the positive qualities God has created in each one of us. Find someone you feel comfortable with to be your partner right now.** (Pause while kids pair up.)

Create a New-You Award for your partner that recognizes one positive quality you see God creating in him or her. For example, you might make a New-You Award for cheerfulness, kindness, commitment to God, patience, friendliness, or something else. You've got two minutes to make your award. Go.

Encourage kids to be creative in the way they make their awards. For example, kids might draw a blue ribbon or gold medal to enhance their awards.

Sound the *squeaker* after two minutes to regain kids' attention. When everyone has responded by raising their hands and focusing on you, have kids present their awards to their partners.

Next have partners take turns answering this question: **What's one important thing you learned today?** (Only God makes us new; God changes us from the inside out; God will forgive our wrongs.)

Conclude by saying: **Take your New-You Award home as a reminder this week that** ☞ **only God makes us new.**

☜ THE **POINT**

TABLE™ TENT

THE WORD on Becoming New and Improved

Monday   Colossians 3:3-10
What's hardest for you about following the instructions of this passage? What can you do about it?

Tuesday   Colossians 3:11
How does new life from Jesus affect the way we treat others?

Wednesday   John 3:3
Why do you think Jesus said this?

Thursday   Ephesians 4:22-24
How would you like others to see God's renewing work in you?

Friday   John 13:34-35
What part does love play in the way God makes us new?

Saturday   Revelation 21:1-5
Describe in your own words what you think the world will be like when God finally makes everything new.

TABLE™ TENT

"If anyone belongs to Christ, there is a new creation. The old things have gone; everything is made new!" (2 Corinthians 5:17).

TABLE™ TENT

TALK TRIGGERS

◆ When do you feel "old and worn out"? When do you feel "new and improved"? Explain.

◆ Tell about someone you know who has really been "made new" by God.

New Life in Christ, Week 6

SHOW-AND-TELL FAITH

THE POINT

☞ **Telling others about God is a privilege.**

THE BIBLE BASIS

Acts 1:8

> But when the Holy Spirit comes to you, you will receive power. You will be my witnesses—in Jerusalem, in all of Judea, in Samaria, and in every part of the world.

Just moments before he ascended into heaven, Jesus communicated his plan for spreading the good news about his life, death, and resurrection. Jesus' followers were to be his heralds, his witnesses to all the earth. The disciples took that commission to be witnesses and literally changed the world with the good news of Christ.

Christian fifth- and sixth-graders need to be reminded that they, too, are Jesus' witnesses. According to recent Group Publishing, Inc. research, only 6 percent of churchgoing fifth- and sixth-graders report talking to their friends about God "often." Nearly half report talking to their friends about God "never or rarely." Kids need to learn to express their faith in creative ways. Use this lesson to teach kids that telling others about Christ can be a terrific, rewarding experience.

This lesson is different in format from other lessons. Kids will prepare presentations to tell others about Christ. During the lesson, they'll go to adult classes to share their presentations.

Contact one or more adult Sunday school classes and ask permission for your kids to make a presentation near the end of class time. Make sure you have one person in each adult class who'll act as a contact person who's responsible for making the kids feel welcome and encouraged. Collect the supplies listed in "This Lesson at a Glance," and you're ready to help your kids experience what it's like to "show and tell" about new life in Christ.

This lesson is structured with the visits to the adult classrooms in mind. If adult classes aren't available, or if you feel your kids would be too uncomfortable doing this, have kids give their presentations for each other instead.

Other Scriptures used in this lesson are **Romans 3:23; 5:6-8, 9-11; 6:23; John 3:16; 10:10;** and **Galatians 5:22-25.**

GETTING THE POINT

Students will
◆ create a presentation that tells others what new life in Christ means to them,
◆ share their faith through a creative presentation, and
◆ discuss what it means to be Jesus' witnesses.

THIS LESSON AT A GLANCE

SECTION	MINUTES	WHAT STUDENTS WILL DO	LEARNING LAB SUPPLIES	CLASSROOM SUPPLIES
GETTING STARTED	5 to 10	**Treat Talks**—Compare talking about a treat to talking about new life in Jesus.		Treats
GETTING GOING	15 to 25	**Preparing to Share**—Examine Acts 1:8 and prepare creative presentations that tell about new life in Christ.	Squeaker, twirlybird, elastic strips, mini straw hat, scented stones, inflatable sword, squeeze ball, carpenter wreath, feather butterfly	Bibles, paper, pencils, newsprint, markers
	10 to 15	**Show and Tell**—Present their faith-sharing messages to adult classes in the church.	Squeaker, twirlybird, elastic strips, mini straw hat, scented stones, inflatable sword, squeeze ball, carpenter wreath, feather butterfly	Bibles
COMING HOME	5 to 10	**Wrapping It Up**—Debrief their experiences in making their presentations and discuss Acts 1:8.		Bibles, refreshments

Remember to make photocopies of the "Table Tent" handout (p. 86) to send home with your kids. The "Table Tent" is a valuable tool for helping fifth- and sixth-graders talk with their parents about what they're learning in class.

THE LESSON

Before the lesson, collect the necessary items from the Learning Lab for the activities you plan to use. Refer to the pictures in the margins to see what each item looks like.

As kids arrive, ask them about last week's "Table Tent" discussion. Use questions such as "What did you learn about your family?" and "What surprised you about your family's reactions?" However, be careful not to embarrass students whose families choose not to use the "Table Tent."

GETTING STARTED

LEARNING LAB

TREAT TALKS

(5 to 10 minutes)

Begin class with a reminder to kids that whenever you sound the *squeaker,* they're to stop what they're doing, raise their hands, and focus on you. Practice the signal two or three times.

Form two groups—group A and group B. Distribute a secret treat (such as sticks of gum or individually wrapped candy) to everyone in group A. Give everyone in group B a different secret treat. Next, have kids pair up with students from the opposite group. Have partners describe their treats to each other without actually naming them. For example, kids might say, "This is sweet and juicy" or "My treat is my favorite kind of candy."

Then ask:

◆ **What was easy or difficult about describing for your partner a treat that he or she hadn't experienced?** (It was easy to compare my treat to something my partner knew about; it was hard because I didn't know exactly how to describe my treat.)

◆ **How is telling a partner about a treat we've received like telling others about the new life we've received from Jesus?** (It helps to describe Jesus in a way others will understand; sometimes telling people about Jesus is difficult because I don't know what to say.)

Say: **It can be interesting to describe a treat, but** 📖 **it's a privilege to tell others about God. We're going to do that today.**

THE **POINT** 📖

GETTING GOING

PREPARING TO SHARE

(15 to 25 minutes)

Have the class read **Acts 1:8** in unison. Ask:

◆ **Why do you think Jesus called his followers his "witnesses"?** (Because they saw what Jesus had done; because Jesus expected his followers to tell others about him.)

◆ **In what ways have you seen or heard people being Jesus' witnesses?** (I have a friend at school who acts the way I think Jesus would; my mom invites her friends at work to come to church.)

◆ **As one of Jesus' witnesses, what would you like to show or tell others about your new life in Christ?** (That Jesus gives me hope; that Jesus helps me live for him each day.)

Say: 👉 **Telling others about God is a privilege, and we can be creative in the way we communicate the news of our faith to others.**

Form presentation groups of no more than four. Construct the groups carefully, with at least one outgoing, leader-type student in each group.

Say: **I've arranged for each of your foursomes to make a group presentation to an adult class in our church. Every person in your group must contribute in some way to the presentation.**

The purpose of your presentations will be to creatively tell others about new life in Christ. To do that, your presentation should cover these three points: (1) What your life would be like without Jesus, (2) What Jesus did for you, and (3) How your lives are different because of Jesus. Let's take a minute now to discuss what we want to say about these points in our presentations.

Write each of the following questions and Scripture references on separate sheets of newsprint. Hang the newsprint on three walls of the room.

◆ **"What would you say your life would be like without Jesus?" (Romans 3:23; Romans 6:23.)**

◆ **"How would you describe what Jesus did for you?" (John 3:16; Romans 5:6-8.)**

◆ **"How would you say your life is different because of Jesus?" (Romans 5:9-11; John 10:10; Galatians 5:22-25.)**

Have each group gather around a different sheet of newsprint. Tell kids to spend a few minutes looking up the

LEARNING LAB

👉 THE POINT

TEACHER TIP

If adult classes aren't available, or if you feel your kids would be too uncomfortable doing this, have kids prepare and perform their presentations for each other instead. If you have new kids in your class or kids whose faith you're not certain of, allow them to take nonspeaking roles in the presentations.

Scriptures and discussing how the passages answer the questions. Have group members also brainstorm ways they've experienced the truth of those Scriptures in their lives.

For example, after kids read and discuss **Romans 3:23,** they might say that they, too, have fallen short of God's standards in areas such as honesty, family relationships, or the way they treat others. Distribute paper and pencils to everyone so kids can record observations from their discussions.

After a few minutes, sound the *squeaker* to pause discussions. When everyone has responded by raising their hands and focusing on you, have groups switch places and begin new discussions. Continue until kids have discussed all the questions on the newsprint.

As kids are discussing, copy the following list of idea starters onto a new sheet of newsprint for kids to use as they shape their creative presentations about new life in Christ:

◆ Skit
◆ Pantomime
◆ Rap
◆ New words to old song
◆ Humorous monologue
◆ Make and illustrate a storybook to read aloud
◆ Tell a parable or a story with a point
◆ Game or activity that makes a point
◆ Interview
◆ Commercial
◆ Letter to a friend that can be read aloud
◆ Newsletter that can be read aloud
◆ Puppet show
◆ Poster or chart
◆ Debate or speech

Sound the *squeaker* to end small-group discussions. When everyone has responded by raising their hands and focusing on you, show kids the list and the following Learning Lab items: the *squeaker, twirlybird, elastic strips, mini straw hat, scented stones, inflatable sword, squeeze ball, carpenter wreath,* and *feather butterfly.* Also make available more paper, pencils, newsprint, and markers.

Say: **Now that you know *what* you want to say about new life in Christ, let's take a few minutes to figure out *how* you want to say it. It's time to take your notes about the things you've been discussing and shape them into a creative presentation for the adult Sunday school classes!**

In your groups, choose one of the idea starters on this list—or make up one of your own—to form your creative presentations. If you'd like to, you can use one of these Learning Lab items as props. You have 10 to 15

TEACHER TIP

If you have more than three groups of students in class, allow a few groups to discuss the same question at the same time.

TEACHER TIP

Tell kids who use the *twirlybird* to remember these safety precautions:

◆ always spin the *twirlybird* in a counterclockwise direction and

◆ don't aim the *twirlybird* at anyone's face or eyes (including their own).

minutes to complete your presentations before going to the adult classes, so get started!

Act as a "floating supervisor" during this part of the lesson. Travel from group to group to check on kids' progress. Help groups define the focus of their presentations and brainstorm creative methods to use. Allow any type of presentation as long as it's in good taste and presents a message around the theme of new life in Christ.

Encourage kids to use the Learning Lab items to give their presentations some life. For example, they could use the *twirlybird* and say, "My faith is like this *twirlybird* because it lifts me up when I'm down." Or "My life is like this *inflatable sword:* Without Jesus filling me like the air fills this sword, I'm just flat and empty." Or "Jesus helps me to be like this *squeeze ball:* When I get squeezed in or dented by problems, he helps me bounce back to my normal self."

Give kids clues for how they might use something from the idea-starter list as well. For example, kids might create a skit about a student who hears about Jesus for the first time; kids might make up a pantomime that acts out Jesus' crucifixion; or kids might use one of the verses they read as the basis for a rap message, with one person reading the rap while others clap and keep time.

Warn kids when only five minutes of preparation time remain. Then sound the *squeaker* to end preparations and to regain the group's attention.

After kids respond by raising their hands and focusing on you, say: **Telling others about God is a privilege. Let's take a minute now to pray and thank God for giving us this privilege today.**

Lead kids in a sort of "commissioning" type of prayer. Thank God for their creative efforts and for the privilege of telling others about new life in Jesus. Then, mentioning students by name, ask God to go with your kids as they make their presentations in the adult classes.

THE POINT

SHOW AND TELL

(10 to 15 minutes)

Tell groups which adult classes they're to make their presentations to and where those classes are meeting. Be sure to give kids the names of the contact people in the adult classes. It's all right if two or more groups present in the same adult class.

Tell kids to introduce their presentations by saying something like "We're from the *(name of class)* here at church. Our

LEARNING LAB

names are *(students' names)*, and we'd like to do a short presentation for you that tells about our new life in Christ." If you'd like, you can have kids write out the introductory statement and take it with them to the adult classes.

Many kids will be nervous—that's OK. Encourage kids by explaining that the adult classes are expecting them and looking forward to their presentations. Also, let kids know that they'll have refreshments to enjoy when they return.

At the prearranged time, send out your presentation groups. Tell kids to synchronize their watches and to be sure to return within 10 to 15 minutes. You may want to accompany kids to the classes and announce them with enthusiasm.

You may also want to move from class to class while kids are presenting so that you can see a minute or two of each group's presentation and cheer them on.

As kids return to the room, collect the Learning Lab items and have everyone work together to clean up the other supplies before moving on to the next activity. Send out a volunteer to round up any "stragglers" who may not have made it back to the room at the designated time.

TABLE™ TENT

We believe Christian education extends beyond the classroom into the home. Photocopy the "Table Tent" handout (p. 86) for this week and send it home with your kids. Encourage kids and parents to use the handout to spark meaningful discussion on this week's topic. Follow up next week by asking kids how their discussions went with their families.

COMING HOME

WRAPPING IT UP

(5 to 10 minutes)

When everyone has returned to the room, pass out refreshments such as punch and cookies or fruit. Form a circle and have groups take turns reporting about their experiences. Lead kids in a round of applause after each report.

Then have everyone read **Acts 1:8** in unison again. Ask:

◆ **How did it feel to tell others about your new life in Christ this way? Explain.** (Great, because I've never done it before; scary, because I was so nervous; exciting, because they were so appreciative.)

◆ **How could this experience prepare you to tell your friends about your new life in Christ this week?** (I have a better idea of what to say; I can be more creative in the way I tell others about Jesus.)

◆ **Why is it important to be Jesus' witnesses and creatively tell others about our new life in Christ?** (So others can get to know Jesus, too; because God counts on us to share the good news.)

◆ **What's one important thing you've learned today?** (Telling others about God is a privilege; I don't have to be afraid to tell others about Jesus; telling others about Jesus can be fun.)

Say:☞**Telling others about God is a privilege. Let's take a minute now to thank our presentation partners for helping us tell about our new life in Christ.**

Have kids re-form their presentation groups and take turns completing this sentence about their partners: "One valuable contribution you made to our presentation was..."

After everyone has finished, dismiss with a standing ovation for kids' efforts during this class.

☜ THE **POINT**

TABLE™ TENT

"You will be my witnesses" (Acts 1:8b).

Talk Triggers

▲ What is the most exciting thing about being a Christian?

▲ Tell what happened the last time you talked about your faith with a friend.

THE WORD on Show-and-Tell Faith

Monday   Matthew 28:16-20
What does this command mean to you?

Tuesday   Luke 24:46-53
How would you have responded if you'd been one of the disciples Jesus spoke these words to? Why?

Wednesday   Mark 16:15
How can you fulfill this verse with your words and actions?

Thursday   John 3:16
When was the last time you told someone about God's love? When's the next time you can tell someone?

Friday   2 Corinthians 5:17
Tell about a time someone recognized that your new life in Christ made you different from others in a good way.

Saturday   2 Timothy 1:7-10
What makes it hard for others to see that you've got new life in Christ? What would make it easier?

WELCOME BACK, JESUS!

THE POINT

☞ **Jesus' return gives us hope.**

THE BIBLE BASIS

1 Thessalonians 4:13-18

> Brothers and sisters, we want you to know about those Christians who have died so you will not be sad, as others who have no hope. We believe that Jesus died and that he rose again. So, because of him, God will raise with Jesus those who have died. What we tell you now is the Lord's own message. We who are living when the Lord comes again will not go before those who have already died. The Lord himself will come down from heaven with a loud command, with the voice of the archangel, and with the trumpet call of God. And those who have died believing in Christ will rise first. After that, we who are still alive will be gathered up with them in the clouds to meet the Lord in the air. And we will be with the Lord forever. So encourage each other with these words.

The Christians of Thessalonica weren't sure what to think about the events surrounding Christ's second coming. They knew Jesus had promised to return, but what would become of those Christians who had died before Christ's coming? In **1 Thessalonians 4:13-18,** Paul addressed this concern with a stirring description of Jesus' return. It promises to be a dramatic, earth-shaking, unprecedented event, bringing new life for both the dead in Christ and the living.

Fifth- and sixth-graders aren't sure what to think about a lot of things. They worry about how to make people like them, how they'll change as they grow up, and whether or not their families will remain stable. Kids sometimes focus on these worries so much that they lose sight of the daily hope found in Jesus' promised return. When the Thessalonians were worried, Paul encouraged them with the news of Christ's second coming. Use this lesson about Christ's return to encourage your students to focus on the hope and joy that awaits all Christians.

Other Scriptures used in the lesson are **Matthew 24:36-39; Matthew 24:42-51;** and **Revelation 22:20.**

GETTING THE POINT

Students will
◆ discuss what Jesus' promised return means to them,
◆ discover how hard it is to make accurate predictions, and
◆ experience an unexpected return.

THIS LESSON AT A GLANCE

SECTION	MINUTES	WHAT STUDENTS WILL DO	LEARNING LAB SUPPLIES	CLASSROOM SUPPLIES
ATTENTION GRABBER	7 to 12	**Deck the Walls**—Decorate the room for a surprise guest.	Inflatable sword	Newsprint, colored markers, masking tape
BIBLE EXPLORATION AND APPLICATION	8 to 13	**Something to Look Forward To**—Respond to interview questions about Jesus' return and discuss 1 Thessalonians 4:13-18.	Cassette: "What Do You Think About Jesus' Return?"	Cassette player, Bibles, newsprint, marker
	8 to 13	**Ready or Not**—Examine Matthew 24:42-51 after trying to complete tasks in time for inspection.	Squeeze ball, squeaker	Bibles, newsprint, marker, paper, pencils, individually wrapped candy
	7 to 12	**Hot Ball**—Make predictions about how a game will turn out and talk about Matthew 24:36-39.	Squeeze ball, Cassette: "Hot Ball"	Bibles, 3×5 cards, pencils, cassette player
CLOSING	5 to 10	**To Jesus!**—Offer "toasts" to celebrate Jesus' promised return.		Bible, beverage, cups

Remember to make photocopies of the "Table Tent" handout (p. 96) to send home with your kids. The "Table Tent" is a valuable tool for helping fifth- and sixth-graders talk with their parents about what they're learning in class.

THE LESSON

Before the lesson, collect the necessary items from the Learning Lab for the activities you plan to use. Refer to the pictures in the margins to see what each item looks like.

As kids arrive, ask them about last week's "Table Tent" discussion. Use questions such as "What did you learn about your family?" and "What surprised you about your family's reactions?" However, be careful not to embarrass students whose families choose not to use the "Table Tent."

ATTENTION GRABBER

DECK THE WALLS

(7 to 12 minutes)

Begin class with a reminder that whenever you sound the *squeaker,* kids are to stop what they're doing, raise their hands, and focus on you. Practice the signal two or three times.

Say: **Today we're going to have a surprise guest. Let's take a few minutes right now to decorate our room in honor of our visitor. We've only got a few minutes to decorate, so let's work quickly to make it as festive and welcoming for our guest as we can.**

Give kids newsprint and colored markers to make welcome posters for the room. Also, have kids tear newsprint into strips and color the strips with dots or stripes to make creative streamers. Allow kids to include any other creative decorations they can make in the time allotted. If kids ask who the guest of honor is, tell them it's a surprise.

Hang the decorations all around the room. Then gather kids in a circle and say: **Our guest of honor is already here. It's Jesus, and he's with us in Spirit every day. But Jesus has also promised to come back one day to take his followers to heaven.**

Blow up the *inflatable sword* and place it in the center of the circle. Ask the following questions one at a time. Give kids a few seconds of "think time," then spin the sword on the floor. When the sword stops spinning, have the kids sitting on either end of the sword answer the question. Repeat the process for each question. Ask:

◆ **What went through your mind as we prepared this room for a visitor?** (I was excited that someone was coming; I wished we could do more to get the room ready; I wondered who the guest was and when he or she would come.)

LEARNING LAB

TEACHER TIP

If you'd like more answers to each question, simply spin the *inflatable sword* again before asking the next question.

THE **POINT**

◆ **How would you have decorated differently if you'd known Jesus was our guest of honor?** (I would've been more careful; I would've done more; I would've made sure everything was perfect.)

◆ **How does the thought of Jesus returning for his followers make you feel? Why?** (Excited, because I can't wait to see him; nervous, because I don't know what to expect; worried that I won't be ready.)

◆ **What do you think Jesus will want to see when he returns?** (People who live for him; people who show love to each other; people waiting to welcome him.)

Retrieve the *inflatable sword* for later use and say: **The thought of having a surprise guest in class is fun, but the thought of Jesus returning is really exciting! Today we're going to talk more about this and about how** Jesus' **return gives us hope.**

LEARNING LAB

BIBLE EXPLORATION AND APPLICATION

SOMETHING TO LOOK FORWARD TO

(8 to 13 minutes)

Say: **Let's listen now to some interviews with kids your age who were asked what their thoughts were about Jesus' return. As we listen, think about how your answers would've been similar to or different from the ones on the tape.**

Play "What Do You Think About Jesus' Return?" from the *cassette.*

After the *cassette* segment, form groups of no more than three and have trios discuss how they might have answered the interview questions. Sound the *squeaker* to end the discussions and wait for kids to respond. Have the oldest person in each trio report his or her group's responses to the first question, the second oldest report answers to the second question, and so on.

Have trios read **1 Thessalonians 4:13-18** and come up with a one-sentence summary of the passage. Then have groups discuss the following questions. Write the questions on newsprint for kids to refer to during discussions. Ask:

◆ **How do you picture Jesus' return?** (Loud trumpets; angels everywhere; people coming out of their graves.)

◆ **Why do you think Paul included this description of Jesus' promised return in this letter to the Thessalonians?** (He wanted to encourage them; he was excited about Jesus coming back.)

◆ **Why do you think Jesus has waited so long before returning to earth?** (He wants to give more people a chance to follow him; the time for his return hasn't come yet.)

◆ **What makes you nervous or worried about Jesus' return?** (Not knowing for sure whether to believe that Jesus will come back; wondering if I'll be included.)

◆ **Verse 18 tells us to encourage each other with the news of Jesus' return. How can we do that this week?** (We can remind each other of our future with Jesus; we can encourage each other not to give up on living our faith because Jesus will reward us when he comes.)

Sound the *squeaker* to regain kids' attention. After everyone responds by raising their hands and focusing on you, say: **Christians have an awesome future to look forward to— life forever with Jesus. Because of that ☞ Jesus' return gives us hope today, tomorrow, and always.**

🦅 THE **POINT**

READY OR NOT 📖

LEARNING LAB

(8 to 13 minutes)

Form groups of no more than four. Show kids the *squeeze ball* and say: **This is no ordinary ball. You can squeeze it** (flatten the ball, then lay it in your palm where everyone can see it), **and approximately 10 seconds later it returns to its original shape.**

For this next activity, your job is to complete a task and freeze before it's time for inspection. I'll shout out a task for groups to perform, then I'll flatten the ball. Inspection time begins when the ball regains its original shape. Whether you finish or not, freeze when you hear the *squeaker*. Then I'll come by to inspect how well you've done. Ready? Let's get started.

Flatten the *squeeze ball* between your palms as you shout out a task. Then say: **Go!** and release the pressure on the ball while kids perform the task.

When the *squeeze ball* has returned to its original shape, sound the *squeaker* and have kids freeze. While kids are frozen, inspect the groups to see which ones were ready before the *squeaker* sounded. Reward kids who finished in time for inspection with a piece of individually wrapped candy.

Listed below are some tasks you can have kids perform. Use any or all of these for this activity, or you can make up your own. However, be sure to use the last task listed here as your final one.

◆ Lie on the floor to form the letter M.

◆ Leapfrog across the room.

◆ Sing "Mary Had a Little Lamb" in a squeaky, little mouse voice, then take a bow.

◆ Give a compliment to someone not in your group, then stand in a circle with your group.

◆ Form a human sculpture of an airplane.

◆ Pretend to pose for a picture with the president. (Don't forget to smile and say "cheese.")

◆ Open your Bibles to **Matthew 24:42-51.**

When kids have their Bibles open, have them read **Matthew 24:42-51** in their groups. Have groups come up with one sentence that summarizes the theme of the passage.

Tell groups to assign the following roles within their foursomes: a recorder who writes down the group's thoughts, a representative who shares the group's thoughts with the class, a reader who'll read the Scriptures, and an encourager who urges everyone to participate in the discussion.

Have groups discuss the following questions. Write the questions on newsprint for kids to refer to during discussions. Ask:

◆ **What's your reaction to what you just did?** (It was fun; it was impossible to finish some of the tasks in time for inspection; I liked finishing in time for inspection because I got a reward.)

◆ **What part did teamwork play in getting your group ready for inspection?** (We did well when we worked together; it was hard for our group to decide who would do what.)

◆ **How was my inspection like or unlike Jesus' return?** (I was never sure when it was going to happen; Jesus won't care whether or not we finished—he'll just want to know we did our best; Jesus will have a better reward for us than a piece of candy.)

◆ **What do you think it means to be ready for Jesus' return?** (To put God first; to live the way Jesus wants us to live.)

◆ **What are some of the things Jesus wants us to be doing until he comes again?** (Praying; helping others; doing our best at whatever we do; showing love to our families; learning more about God.)

◆ **This week, how can we work as a team to help each other be ready for Jesus' return?** (We can pray for each other; we can remind each other of what we're learning today; we can encourage each other.)

After a few minutes, sound the *squeaker* to end the small-group discussions. When everyone has responded by raising their hands and focusing on you, have the representatives take turns telling how their groups responded.

Say: **For my inspection in this activity, I wanted you to finish your tasks. But we'll never finish the work Jesus has for us to do. According to Matthew 24:42-51, Jesus simply wants to find us doing our best for him when he returns. That's just another reason that ☞ Jesus' return gives us hope.**

🐍 THE **POINT**

HOT BALL

(7 to 12 minutes)

LEARNING LAB

Form a circle and show kids the *squeeze ball*. Tell kids they're going to play a game of Hot Ball, a modified version of Hot Potato. Here are the rules:

■ The object of the game is to toss the *squeeze ball* from person to person within the circle until the music stops.

■ Before throwing the *squeeze ball,* players must call out the name of the person to receive it and a positive word that begins with the first letter of that person's name. For example, kids might call out, "Andy Awesome!" or "Frances Friendly" before throwing the *squeeze ball*.

■ After they've received the *squeeze ball,* kids must sit down and throw it to someone who is still standing. When everyone is seated, kids can stand up and start over.

When everyone understands the rules, distribute 3×5 cards and pencils to everyone. Say: **Before we begin, I'd like you to predict who will end up holding the *squeeze ball* when the music stops.**

Write your prediction on your card without letting anyone see what you've written. (Pause) **Now fold your card and put it in your pocket or shoe while we play the game. We'll play several rounds, so if your prediction doesn't come true the first time, it still might come true later.**

Collect the pencils. Then begin the game by playing "Hot Ball" from the *cassette*. Each time the tape segment pauses, stop the cassette player and see who got caught holding the *squeeze ball*. Check to see if anyone's prediction came true, then restart the cassette player. There are a total of four pauses within the song.

TEACHER TIP

If the music ends before everyone has had an opportunity to receive and throw the ball, quickly rewind the *cassette* and continue the game. Stop when everyone has received the ball at least once.

Afterward, retrieve the *squeeze ball* and put away the *cassette*. Form two concentric circles so that the people in the inner circle are facing the people in the outer circle.

Say: **Discuss your answers to the following question with the person facing you in the other circle. Move one space to the right to get a new discussion partner for each new question.**

Ask:

◆ **What do you think of our predictions for this game?** (They were pretty much wild guesses; I was impressed that anyone could make the right prediction.)

◆ **How are the predictions we made about the game like predictions people make about when Jesus will return?** (People's predictions about Jesus' return are really just guesses, too; people's predictions about Jesus' return usually won't come true either.)

◆ **If you knew that Jesus wouldn't come back to earth for 50 more years, how would that influence the way you live?** (I'd make plans to accomplish all I wanted to before Jesus came back; I might not worry much about being ready until Jesus' return was closer.)

◆ **If you knew that Jesus was coming back tomorrow, how would that influence the way you live?** (I wouldn't do my homework; I'd pray and try to do things that Jesus would be pleased to see when he comes; I'd tell all my friends to get ready.)

Have the outer circle read **Matthew 24:36-39** in unison. Then ask:

◆ **Why do people try to predict the day Jesus will return, when Matthew 24:36-39 tells us that no one knows when it'll be?** (People are curious; people think it's a secret they should figure out; people don't like not knowing.)

◆ **Why do you think God doesn't tell us exactly when Jesus will return?** (God wants us to live every day as if Jesus were going to return that day; God doesn't want us to neglect our everyday responsibilities.)

◆ **How does not being able to predict when Jesus will return affect the way you live?** (It makes me want to be ready every day; it helps me not worry about it.)

◆ **What specific things can you do this week to prepare for Jesus' return?** (Live each day with the attitude that Jesus might come back today; study the Bible to grow closer to God; do my best at whatever I do.)

Sound the *squeaker* to regain kids' attention and wait for them to respond by raising their hands and focusing on you. Have kids take turns telling one new insight they've gained from their discussions.

Then say: **Whether Jesus returns today or 100 years from today isn't really important. What's important is that he will return and that ⟐ Jesus' return gives us hope.**

Put away the *squeeze ball* and the *cassette* for later use.

⟐ THE **POINT**

TABLE™
TENT

W e believe Christian education extends beyond the classroom into the home. Photocopy the "Table Tent" handout (p. 96) for this week and send it home with your kids. Encourage kids and parents to use the handout to spark meaningful discussion on this week's topic. Follow up next week by asking kids how their discussions went with their families.

CLOSING

TO JESUS!

(5 to 10 minutes)

Form a circle and have kids take turns responding to this question: **What's one thing you've learned today that you'd like your friends to know?** (That Jesus' return gives us hope; that we need to be ready for Jesus to return at any time.)

Bring out cups and a favorite beverage, such as punch, orange juice, or Kool-Aid. Form a circle and read aloud **Revelation 22:20.**

Say: **People often welcome a special event with a toast to celebrate the joy that event brings. Because ⟐ Jesus' return gives us hope, I'd like to propose a toast right now to celebrate Jesus and his promise to return for us. This toast will be our prayer of closing today.**

⟐ THE **POINT**

Serve everyone a cup of your chosen beverage, but tell them not to drink it yet. When everyone has a cup, have kids practice this toast based on **Revelation 22:20.**

Say: **To Jesus, who is coming soon.**

Have kids respond by saying, "Amen. Come, Lord Jesus!"

When everyone is ready, dismiss by having kids raise their cups and offer the toast.

"The Lord himself will come down from heaven with a loud command, with the voice of the archangel, and with the trumpet call of God" (1 Thessalonians 4:16a).

Talk Triggers

◆ What does Jesus' promise to return for his followers mean to you? Explain.

◆ Why is it good to remember Jesus' promise to return?

THE WORD on Jesus' Return

Monday   1 Thessalonians 4:13-14
Who are you looking forward to seeing in heaven? Why?

Tuesday   1 Thessalonians 4:15-18
How can your family creatively use this Scripture to encourage someone?

Wednesday   Matthew 24:3-5
How can you follow Jesus' advice in this passage?

Thursday   Matthew 24:36
What predictions have you heard about "the end of the world"? What do you think of them?

Friday   Revelation 22:20
When was the last time you prayed for Jesus to return? What prompted you to pray that?

Saturday   Matthew 25:1-13
What do you think Jesus wants you to learn about his return from this parable?

New Life in Christ, Week 8

(fold here)

BIBLE BASICS

THE POINT

📖 **God's Word is our guidebook for new life.**

THE BIBLE BASIS

Hebrews 4:12

> God's word is alive and working and is sharper than a double-edged sword. It cuts all the way into us, where the soul and the spirit are joined, to the center of our joints and bones. And it judges the thoughts and feelings in our hearts.

This passage in Hebrews makes it clear that God's Word is not a rusty, blunt, obsolete instrument of by-gone days. It's relevant, sharper than a double-edged sword, and active in the lives of people today. By the power of God's spoken word, the universe came into being. And through God's written Word—the Bible—God gives us the power to know and serve him.

Fifth- and sixth-graders may be video game wizards, but they're likely to be at a loss when it comes to using and understanding Scripture. They know they should read and apply the Bible to their lives, but they don't always know how. Use this lesson to teach students Bible skills and to help them experience God's Word as their own, daily guidebook for new life.

Second Timothy 3:16-17 and various other Scriptures are also used in this lesson.

GETTING THE POINT

Students will
◆ learn a song to help them remember the books of the Bible,
◆ discover ways the Bible arms them for life,
◆ become familiar with the types of writing in the Bible, and
◆ practice using a concordance.

THIS LESSON AT A GLANCE

SECTION	MINUTES	WHAT STUDENTS WILL DO	LEARNING LAB SUPPLIES	CLASSROOM SUPPLIES
ATTENTION GRABBER	7 to 12	**Bible Bounce**—Learn a song to help them remember the books of the Bible.	Cassette: "The Holy Books," lyrics poster	Bible, cassette player, pencils
BIBLE EXPLORATION AND APPLICATION	8 to 13	**On Guard!**—Participate in a mock duel and discuss Hebrews 4:12.	Inflatable sword, feather butterfly	Bibles, masking tape
	8 to 13	**Card Catalog of the Bible**—Use Scriptures to identify the different writing styles included in the Bible.		Bibles, "Card Catalog of the Bible" handout (p. 107)
	8 to 13	**Conquer That Concordance**—Examine 2 Timothy 3:16-17 after they practice using a concordance.		Bibles, concordances, paper, pencils
CLOSING	2 to 7	**The Holy Books**—Review the books of the Bible by singing "The Holy Books."	Cassette: "The Holy Books," lyrics poster	Cassette player
MODULE REVIEW	3 to 7	**Reflection**—Review what they've learned over the past five lessons.		
Remember to make photocopies of the "Table Tent" handout (p. 108) to send home with your kids. The "Table Tent" is a valuable tool for helping fifth- and sixth-graders talk with their parents about what they're learning in class.				

THE LESSON

Before the lesson, collect the necessary items from the Learning Lab for the activities you plan to use. Refer to the pictures in the margins to see what each item looks like.

As kids arrive, ask them about last week's "Table Tent" discussion. Use questions such as "What did you learn about your family?" and "What surprised you about your family's reactions?" However, be careful not to embarrass students whose families choose not to use the "Table Tent."

ATTENTION GRABBER

BIBLE BOUNCE

(7 to 12 minutes)

Begin class with a reminder to kids that whenever you sound the *squeaker*, they're to stop what they're doing, raise their hands, and focus on you. Practice the signal two or three times.

Say: **Today we're going to learn about the Bible because God's Word is our guidebook for new life. The first step to using a guidebook is simply to know what's in it. So, we're going to start this class by learning a new song that'll help us remember what books are included in the Bible.**

Form a circle. Give each person a pencil and a photocopy of the table of contents from a Bible. (Be sure the table of contents includes both the Old and New Testaments.)

Moving around the circle in order, assign each student the name of a book of the Bible. Go around as many times as needed until all 66 books are assigned. Have kids write their initials next to the books they're assigned so they'll remember them during the activity.

Hold up the *lyrics poster* to show kids the words to "The Holy Books." Keep the poster in a prominent place during the activity so kids can refer to it if they want to.

Say: **The song we're going to learn lists the books of the Bible in order. First, we'll listen to it all the way through. Then we'll play it again and sing along. The second time through, when you hear the name of your book, stand up, clap your hands, and sit down as fast as you can. We'll see if we can make it through the song the second time without having more than one person standing at a time.**

LEARNING LAB

THE POINT

TEACHER TIP

Assign 1, 2, and 3 John all to one person and 1 and 2 Peter both to another person because the song you'll be using ("The Holy Books") puts these books together.

As you're assigning the books of the Bible, point out where each book is in the table of contents and say the book name aloud. That'll help kids who're unfamiliar with the spelling or pronunciation of Bible names.

Play "The Holy Books" on the *cassette* to begin the activity. It's recorded twice in a row for your convenience. Encourage kids to follow along with the words the first time through and to sing along the second time through.

When the song is over, turn off the *cassette* and ask:

◆ **Why do you think it's important to know the books of the Bible?** (Because knowing the order of the books makes it easier to find things in the Bible; because knowing what's in the Bible makes the Bible less confusing.)

THE **POINT**

Say: **We'll sing this song again later in this lesson. It's good to learn what's in the Bible because** **God's Word is our guidebook for new life. Let's see what else we can learn about the Bible today.**

Have kids put away their tables of contents. Leave the *lyrics poster* up throughout the rest of the lesson.

BIBLE EXPLORATION AND APPLICATION

LEARNING LAB

ON GUARD!

(8 to 13 minutes)

Use masking tape to mark a large circle on the floor. Form two teams—team A and team B. Have each team gather on opposite sides of the circle.

Tell kids it's time for a "duel" and ask for one volunteer from each team to step into the circle.

Say: **The object of this duel is to see which team member can be the first to touch the other with his or her sword. Both volunteers must stay inside the circle at all times. We'll have new volunteers after each duel until everyone has had a chance to play.**

Give the *inflatable sword* to team A's volunteer. To the other volunteer, say: **Since I don't have another *inflatable sword*, team B will have to use the *feather butterfly* as a sword instead.**

Despite kids' objections, give the second volunteer the *feather butterfly* and start the duels. Keep track of the number of wins for each team and caution kids not to get too aggressive.

Afterward, retrieve the *inflatable sword* and *feather butterfly*. Have kids choose a discussion partner from the opposing team. Ask kids the following questions, pausing after each one to allow time for partners to discuss their answers. Have kids report any insights they'd like to share after discussing each question. Ask:

◆ **What did you think of our duels?** (I didn't like them because they were unfair; I felt sorry for the team with the butterfly; I wish I could've used the *inflatable sword*.)

◆ **How did your advantage or disadvantage affect the way you fought during the duels?** (I wasn't afraid to attack; I tried to run away.)

Have one person in each pair read **Hebrews 4:12** and the other summarize it in one sentence. Ask:

◆ **Why do you think Hebrews 4:12 compares the Bible to a sword?** (It can cut through to our thoughts and feelings; it's a powerful weapon.)

◆ **How is trying to duel with the** *feather butterfly* **for a sword like trying to duel life's problems without the sword of God's Word?** (It's hard to defend yourself; you can be overpowered easily.)

◆ **How can the Bible help us?** (It gives us a strong weapon against evil; it gives us confidence to live for God; it helps us overcome fear.)

◆ **What do you need to do to use God's Word?** (Read it more; get a better understanding of how to use it; practice what I learn from the Bible.)

Say: **The** *inflatable sword* **wouldn't have done much good if team A had set it on a shelf and refused to use it. Likewise, our Bibles aren't much use if we set them on the shelf and ignore them.** ☞ **God's Word is our guidebook for new life. We need to become familiar with our Bibles so we can become good "swordsmen and women" of God's Word.**

⅃ THE POINT

CARD CATALOG OF THE BIBLE 📖

(8 to 13 minutes)

Distribute photocopies of the "Card Catalog of the Bible" handout (p. 107).

Say: **The Bible communicates God's love and expectations for us. On your handout, the books of the Bible are grouped according to their topic or category. Take a moment to look over your handout now.**

After kids have had time to read their handouts, form groups of no more than four. Have kids number off from one to four within their groups. Say: **Now we're going to play a** game. I'm going to read a Scripture, then I'd like your group to guess which category on your handout that Scripture fits into. After 10 to 15 seconds, I'll call out a number from one to four. The person in your group whose number I call out will be responsible for reporting your answer.

Read aloud the following Scripture passages one at a time but <u>don't reveal the references for the passages</u>. After 15 seconds or so, have the designated students tell the categories their groups chose and why. Then give kids the Scripture reference and have everyone shout out the correct category based on where the book is on their handouts.

Use these Scriptures: **John 14:6** (Gospels); **Exodus 20:7** (Law); **Psalm 119:105** (Poetic books); **2 Samuel 5:4-5** (Old Testament historical book); **Acts 12:1-3** (New Testament historical book); **Isaiah 62:11** (Old Testament prophetic book); **1 Corinthians 1:1-2** (Letter of Paul).

Afterward, have groups answer these questions:

◆ **Why do you think there are so many different types of books in the Bible?** (So it will appeal to all kinds of people; to help us understand God in different ways.)

◆ **What did you learn about God or God's Word in this activity?** (Jesus is the only way to God; the Bible is like a lamp that gives us guidance.)

◆ **How can knowing the different categories of books help you understand the Bible better?** (It can help me recognize historical examples and learn from them; it can help me understand why Psalms uses poetic language; it can help me read Paul's writings like letters.)

◆ **What can you do this week to become more familiar with the way the Bible is written?** (Begin reading all the books in a specific category; compare what's written in different parts of the Bible.)

Say: **Understanding the way the Bible is written helps make it easier to understand and apply God's Word in our daily lives. Put your handout in your Bible now and take it home for future reference. Let it be a reminder to you that God's Word is our guidebook for new life.**

TEACHER TIP

If you're running short on time, you may want to eliminate some of the Scriptures for this activity. If you have extra time, feel free to add Scriptures of your choice.

THE **POINT**

CONQUER THAT CONCORDANCE

(8 to 13 minutes)

If you skipped the previous activity, form groups of no more than four and have group members number off. Make sure each group has a Bible. You'll also need a concordance (or a Bible with a concordance in the back) for each group.

Say: **We're going to do a "Conquer That Concordance" exercise. A concordance is a reference book that helps you find what you're looking for in the Bible.**

For example, suppose you wanted to find "The Lord is my shepherd" in the Bible, but you couldn't remember where it was. You could look up "shepherd" in the concordance. Once you found "shepherd," you'd see a whole list of verses that use the word. So you'd need to read through the list until you found "The Lord is my shepherd." Let's try that now.

Hand a concordance to the ones in each group and have groups use their concordances to find the reference for "The Lord is my Shepherd."

When groups are ready, have everyone shout out the response to the question: "Where is 'The Lord is my shepherd' found in the Bible?" **(Psalm 23:1.)**

Say: **We're halfway there—we know where to find the verse. Now we just have to look it up. Find Psalm 23:1 in your Bible.**

Pause while kids look up the verse. Then say: **Congratulations! You've just used a concordance to help you find guidance from God's Word.**

Now, suppose you don't have a specific verse in mind, but you want to find out what the Bible has to say about a general topic, like love. You can use a concordance to look up the word "love" and then look up any of the verses listed. Or maybe you want to know where to read about a certain person, such as Moses. What could you do? Look up "Moses" in the concordance, then check out the passages listed.

Tell kids to give the concordances to the twos in their groups and the Bibles to the fours.

Say: **All right. We're ready for "Conquer That Concordance." Here's how it works.**

I'm going to call out either a specific Bible quotation or a general topic. The person holding the concordance must use it to find the appropriate Scripture reference. Then the person holding the Bible must open it to that passage. Then we'll have the Bible holders stand and read their Scriptures for the class.

Start when kids understand the rules. Use your own concordance to check answers and have group members take turns holding the concordances and Bibles. If kids are all looking up the same verse, have the Bible holders read their passages in unison. For general topics, kids might come up with different verses, so have Bible holders take turns reading aloud

TEACHER TIP

Note any potentially confusing features of the concordances you have and explain them to the kids.

For example, most concordances use only the first letter of the key word when they write out the verse portion. So, "The Lord is my shepherd" would be written "The Lord is my s." Also, help kids decipher abbreviations for the books of the Bible.

TEACHER TIP

The specific verses are harder to find than the general topics or people because kids have to decide which word to look up, then read through the options. If you see that a student holding a Bible is one who has trouble reading, don't ask for a specific verse; ask for a general topic instead. But do end with **2 Timothy 3:16,** since you will be discussing this verse.

their Scriptures instead. Use these instructions for the contest.

◆ Find any verse about this general topic in the Bible: hope.

◆ Find this specific verse in the Bible: "Clap your hands, all you people." **(Psalm 47:1.)**

◆ Find any verse about this person in the Bible: Ruth.

◆ Find any verse about this general topic in the Bible: joy.

◆ Find any verse about this general topic in the Bible: friends.

◆ Find any verse about this person in the Bible: Jesus.

◆ Find this specific verse in the Bible: "All Scripture is given by God." **(2 Timothy 3:16.)**

Say: **Keep your finger in the Bible at the last passage we looked up—2 Timothy 3:16.**

Applaud the winning team and congratulate both teams for having learned a new skill.

Tell groups to assign the following roles within their foursomes: a recorder who writes down the group's thoughts, a representative who shares the group's thoughts with the class, a reader who'll read **2 Timothy 3:16-17,** and an encourager who urges everyone to participate in the discussion.

Give paper and pencils to the recorders. Then have groups come up with one-sentence summaries of **2 Timothy 3:16-17** and report their summaries to the class. Ask:

◆ **What feelings did you have during the contest? Explain.** (I was nervous that I wouldn't be able to find my passage; I was excited because our team was doing well; I was stressed because I've never done this kind of thing before.)

Pause for discussion after each question. Before moving on to the next question, allow kids to share any insights they've gained from their discussions.

◆ **How are those feelings like the way you feel when you need guidance from the Bible?** (I get excited when I find guidance from the Bible; I get stressed when I can't find what I need in the Bible.)

◆ **Why do you think 2 Timothy 3:16-17 gives this description of the Bible?** (To remind us that God's Word is our guide for new life; to encourage us to rely on God's Word.)

◆ **What makes it hard for you to find the guidance that 2 Timothy 3:16-17 promises is in the Bible?** (I don't know where to look; I don't understand what I'm reading.)

THE POINT ☞

Say: ☞**God's Word is our guidebook for new life, and a concordance can help us use that guidebook more easily. Now that you know how to use a concordance, I encourage you to practice using it this week and in the weeks to come.**

Before moving to the closing, tell kids you'd like to take

one minute to recognize ways they've contributed to the class so far.

Say: **Complete this sentence with one positive word and a description that fits your partner. "(Person's name), if your name were in a concordance, it'd be under (blank) because..."**

For example, "Roni, if your name were in a concordance, it'd be under 'cheerfulness' because you have a great attitude" or "Taylor, if your name were in a concordance, it'd be under 'friend' because you're so helpful to others."

TABLE™ TENT

We believe Christian education extends beyond the classroom into the home. Photocopy the "Table Tent" handout (p. 108) for this week and send it home with your kids. Encourage kids and parents to use the handout to spark meaningful discussion on this week's topic. Follow up next week by asking kids how their discussions went with their families.

CLOSING

THE HOLY BOOKS

(3 to 7 minutes)

Quickly rewind the *cassette* to the beginning of the second "Holy Books" song. Have everyone stand and face you as you hold up the *lyrics poster.*

Say: **We're going to review the books of the Bible one more time with the song "The Holy Books." First let's sing it through with the *cassette.* Then let's see if we can do it without depending on the *cassette.* I'll put the *cassette* away, and we'll sing using only the *lyrics poster.* Ready? Let's go!**

Lead kids in singing "The Holy Books." Encourage kids to keep singing even if they make mistakes.

Afterward, congratulate everyone and say: **You've learned a lot about the Bible today! And it will be useful for as long as you live because**  **God's Word is our guidebook for new life.**

LEARNING LAB

THE **POINT**

MODULE REVIEW

REFLECTION

(3 to 7 minutes)

Say: **Think for a moment about what you've learned today and during the previous four class sessions. Be ready to share your thoughts.**

After a minute of "think time," form pairs and have partners take turns completing these sentences:

◆ "The most important thing I've learned from these five class sessions is . . . "

◆ "One thing I've done differently because of what I've learned in this class is . . . "

◆ "One Scripture from these five class sessions that's encouraged me is . . . "

◆ "One thing I'd like to tell my friends about this class is . . . "

Before dismissing class, sound the *squeaker* to regain kids' attention. When everyone has responded by raising their hands and focusing on you, have pairs report how they completed any one of the sentences above.

Card Catalog of the Bible

The Bible communicates God's love and expectations for us through many different types of books.

Refer to the "card catalog" below to help you recognize the different categories of books in the Bible.

Old Testament

Malachi
Zechariah
Haggai
Zephaniah
Habakkuk
Nahum
Micah
Jonah
Obadiah
Amos
Joel
Hosea / MINOR PROPHETS
Daniel
Ezekiel
Lamentations
Jeremiah
Isaiah / MAJOR PROPHETS
Books of Prophecy
Song of Solomon
Ecclesiastes
Proverbs
Psalms
Job **Books of Poetry**
Esther
Nehemiah
Ezra
2 Chronicles
1 Chronicles
2 Kings
1 Kings
2 Samuel
1 Samuel
Ruth
Judges
Joshua **Books of History**
Deuteronomy
Numbers
Leviticus
Exodus
Genesis **Books of God's Law**

New Testament

Revelation
Book of Prophecy
Jude
3 John
2 John
1 John
2 Peter
1 Peter
James
Hebrews **Other Letters to Early Christians**
Philemon
Titus
2 Timothy
1 Timothy
2 Thessalonians
1 Thessalonians
Colossians
Philippians
Ephesians
Galatians
2 Corinthians
1 Corinthians
Romans **Letters by Paul to Early Christians**
Acts **The History of the Early Church**
John
Luke
Mark
Matthew
The Gospels/The History of Jesus's Life on Earth

Panel 1

TABLE™ TENT

THE WORD on Bible Basics

Monday 2 Timothy 3:14-15
How do the Scriptures lead us to "salvation through faith in Christ Jesus"?

Tuesday Psalm 119:1-2
In what ways does following God's teaching in the Bible make a person happy?

Wednesday Psalm 119:16
Which of the Bible's guidelines do you enjoy following? Why?

Thursday Psalm 119:37
What distracts you from the Bible and its teaching?

Friday Psalm 119:105
Why do you think God's Word is compared to a lamp? What else could you compare it to?

Saturday 2 Timothy 3:16-17
What's one thing you've learned from God's Word this week?

····· (fold here) ·····

Panel 2

TABLE™ TENT

"God's word is . . . sharper than a double-edged sword" (Hebrews 4:12).

Holy Bible

For some reason, Corey noticed it had been awhile since he last read his Bible.

····· (fold here) ·····

Panel 3

TABLE™ TENT

TALK TRIGGERS

◆ What contemporary item would you use to describe God's Word? Why?

◆ How can God's Word defend you? How can you use it to go on the offensive against evil?

New Life in Christ, Week 9
Permission to photocopy this handout granted for local church use.
Copyright © Group Publishing, Inc., Box 481, Loveland, CO 80539.

SUCCESS AND FAILURE

BY
DR. DAVE GALLAGHER AND
DEBORAH C. WOMELSDUFF

By all accounts, Charles was a loser. He was uncoordinated in sports, struggled to pass his classes (he eventually failed them all in eighth grade), and was too scared to ask a girl out for a date. But Charles M. Schulz turned his failures into an internationally successful cartoon character named Charlie Brown. The rest is history.

At one time or another, every fifth- or sixth-grader has felt like Charles M. Schulz and Charlie Brown. Painfully aware of their mistakes, kids can be quick to brand themselves as losers. Gina feels like a failure because she has trouble making friends. Ty plays third string on the school football team. Sandy can't resist the temptation to binge on chocolate, even though she's overweight. And Kenyon lacks the confidence to try anything new.

Fifth- and sixth-graders need to know that God doesn't see them as losers. God views them as his children, people uniquely created in God's image and for God's purpose. Understanding that can help kids deal positively with the "wins" and "losses" in life. Use these four lessons to help your "Charlie Browns" discover what success means from an eternal perspective.

━ FOUR LESSONS ON SUCCESS AND FAILURE ━

LESSON	PAGE	THE POINT	THE BIBLE BASIS
10—Gold Medal Friendships	111	We make friends by caring about others.	Romans 13:8-10
11—The Agony of Defeat	123	God can make our failures stepping stones to success.	Luke 22:54-62
12—Reaching for Heaven	137	True success is becoming like Jesus.	Philippians 1:20
13—Be-Awesome Attitudes	149	God's people can be positive and joyful regardless of the circumstance.	Philippians 1:3-6

LEARNING LAB

THE SIGNAL

During the lessons on Success and Failure, your signal to get kids' attention will be to squeeze the *squeaker* found in the Learning Lab. In response to the *squeaker,* have kids immediately stop what they're doing, raise their hands, and focus on you.

Tell kids about this signal—and practice it—before the lesson begins. Explain that it's important to respond to this signal quickly so the class can do as many fun activities as possible. During the lessons, you'll be prompted when to use the signal.

LEARNING LAB

THE TIME STUFFER

This module's Time Stuffer is the *Tips for Success* poster. This poster will help kids think of creative ways to act on what they're learning in class.

Hang the poster in a prominent place in the room and place pens or pencils nearby. During free moments before or after class, kids can read the ideas on the left side of the poster, then write their own tips for success on the right side.

GOLD MEDAL FRIENDSHIPS

THE POINT

☞ **We make friends by caring about others.**

THE BIBLE BASIS

Romans 13:8-10

Do not owe people anything, except always owe love to each other, because the person who loves others has obeyed all the law. The law says, "You must not be guilty of adultery. You must not murder anyone. You must not steal. You must not want to take your neighbor's things." All these commands and all others are really only one rule: "Love your neighbor as you love yourself." Love never hurts a neighbor. So loving is obeying all the law.

You rarely hear someone say, "Get into debt and stay there!" But when it comes to loving others, that's the command Paul gave to Christians. Our obligation to love others should be treated as a never-ending debt, payable each day we live. In this way, Christians can fulfill all of God's commands for inter-personal relationships.

Many fifth- and sixth-graders fall short when it comes to ful-filling God's command to "love your neighbor as yourself." As much as kids desire solid friendships, they often don't know what it means to be a friend. They confuse loving others with being loved and having friends with being popular. Kids need help in understanding that true friendship is "others-centered" and rooted in love. Use this lesson to encourage fifth- and sixth-graders to pay their friends the "debt of love" described in **Romans 13:8-10.**

Other Scriptures used in the lesson are **Hebrews 10:24; Philippians 4:8;** and **Matthew 7:12.**

GETTING THE POINT

Students will
- ◆ incur a debt of love and act to fulfill that debt,
- ◆ discuss how to respond when friends want them to do wrong, and
- ◆ learn how to give meaningful encouragement to a friend.

THIS LESSON AT A GLANCE

SECTION	MINUTES	WHAT STUDENTS WILL DO	LEARNING LAB SUPPLIES	CLASSROOM SUPPLIES
ATTENTION GRABBER	7 to 12	**May the Best Friend Win**—Plan a campaign for "The Best Friend."		Paper, pencils, markers, newsprint
BIBLE EXPLORATION AND APPLICATION	8 to 13	**Tongue Twister Debts**—Examine Romans 12:8-10 after playing a game where they each incur a debt of love.		Bibles, "Debt Cards" handout (p. 121), cellophane tape, snacks
	8 to 13	**Good Friends, Good Deeds**—Explore solutions to a recorded drama about friends and discuss Hebrews 10:24.	Cassette: "Good Friends, Good Deeds"	Bibles, paper, pencils, cassette player
	7 to 12	**Phony Encouragement**—Compare ridiculously phony compliments to sincere encouragement and talk about Philippians 4:8.	Gold medallions	Bibles, 3×5 cards, pencils
CLOSING	5 to 10	**The Golden Rule**—Trade stories about how others have been caring friends to them.	Mini straw hat	3×5 cards, pencils

Remember to make photocopies of the "Table Tent" handout (p. 122) to send home with your kids. The "Table Tent" is a valuable tool for helping fifth- and sixth-graders talk with their parents about what they're learning in class.

THE LESSON

Before the lesson, collect the necessary items from the Learning Lab for the activities you plan to use. Refer to the pictures in the margins to see what each item looks like.

As kids arrive, ask them about last week's "Table Tent" discussion. Use questions such as "What did you learn about your family?" and "What surprised you about your family's reactions?" However, be careful not to embarrass students whose families choose not to use the "Table Tent."

ATTENTION GRABBER

MAY THE BEST FRIEND WIN

(7 to 12 minutes)

Begin class with a reminder to kids that whenever you sound the *squeaker,* they're to stop what they're doing, raise their hands, and focus on you. Practice the signal two or three times.

Say: **Today we're going to talk about what it means to be a "gold medal" friend. To do that, let's start with an activity that will help us explore some important aspects of friendship.**

Form two groups and distribute paper, pencils, markers, and newsprint to each group. Tell kids they've just become campaign staffers in the election for "The Best Friend." Have the first group prepare a campaign for Patty Popular and the second group prepare one for Fred Friendly.

Say: **As a campaign staff, your responsibilities are (1) to write a short speech for your candidate, (2) to create a campaign button, and (3) to make a campaign poster advertising your candidate. Think about the characteristics of a popular person or a friendly person, then prepare your campaign accordingly.**

For example, a campaign for Patty Popular might point out that everyone in the whole school knows her, that everyone wants to be her friend anyway, and that only unpopular people wouldn't vote for her because they're jealous. A campaign for Fred Friendly might tell about the nice things he does for people, how loyal he is, and how he's fun to be around. You have four minutes to prepare your campaigns. Go!

After four minutes, sound the *squeaker* to draw kids back together. When everyone responds by raising their hands and

LEARNING LAB

TEACHER TIP

Encourage kids to divide responsibilities within their groups. For example, one or two students could work on the campaign speech, others could make campaign buttons, and the rest would create campaign posters.

If students are worried about writing a campaign speech in such a short time, tell them to have their speeches answer the question "Why should you vote for this candidate?"

focusing on you, have each group select a volunteer to give the campaign speech to the class. Have the rest of that group's campaign staff cheer and display their posters and buttons during the speeches.

Applaud both groups afterward. Then ask:

◆ **What was easy or difficult for you in this activity?** (It was easy to think of reasons to vote for a friendly person; it was hard to think of reasons to vote for Patty besides telling everyone she's popular.)

◆ **What did you notice about the two campaigns?** (Fred's campaign talked about all he does for others; Patty's campaign talked about belonging to the "in" group.)

◆ **Would you rather be known as popular or friendly? Why?** (Popular, because then I'd be important and everyone would like me; friendly, because I could just be myself without worrying about what others thought.)

◆ **Besides popularity and friendliness, what qualities did you think were important to bring out about your candidates?** (We wanted Fred to be known as a loyal friend; we wanted Patty to be known as someone who takes time to be there for her friends.)

Say: **When it comes to friendship, it doesn't really matter whether you're popular or not. What matters is the kind of friend you are. Today we're going to learn more about how 📖 we make friends by caring for others.**

TEACHER TIP

It's important to say The Point just as it's written in each activity. Repeating The Point over and over throughout the lesson will help kids remember it and apply it to their lives.

THE **POINT** 📖

BIBLE EXPLORATION AND APPLICATION

▮ TONGUE TWISTER DEBTS   📖

(8 to 13 minutes)

Before class, photocopy and cut apart the "Debt Cards" handout on page 121. Make sure you have at least one card for each person. Fold the cards and tape them shut so that only the words "Debt Card" are visible. Then place the cards in a pile nearby. You'll also need snacks, such as doughnut holes or strawberries.

Have kids stand and form a circle.

Say: **We're going to play a game called Tongue Twister Debts. For this game, we'll take turns saying, "Unique New York" five times in three seconds or less. Whoever**

doesn't say it correctly in the time allotted must draw a debt card. After we're all done, anyone holding a debt card must do what's written on it. Ready? Let's go!

Time students as they attempt to say the tongue twister. If anyone does successfully complete the tongue twister in the allotted time, have him or her try saying it 10 times in three seconds.

After everyone has incurred a "debt," have kids follow the instructions on their cards to "pay their debts." Then re-form the circle for the next series of questions and have kids put their right feet inside the circle.

Have kids take turns sharing their responses to each question. When one student shares an answer, allow anyone who thought of the same answer—and has nothing more to add—to remove his or her foot from the circle. When all feet are removed, ask the next question and repeat the process. Ask:

◆ **What did you think about having to draw a debt card?** (At first I was worried about what I'd have to do; after I saw what the debt was, I hoped I would be the next to draw one.)

◆ **What were you thinking as you "paid your debts" and received payment from your friends?** (I was glad to get a snack; I hoped everyone would get a snack; I wanted to give a snack to the person who gave me one.)

Have everyone read **Romans 13:8-10** in unison. Then ask:

◆ **How would you summarize the theme of this passage?** (We should always love each other; loving others fulfills God's law.)

◆ **How did our actions during the game communicate the message of Romans 13:8-10?** (We showed love to each other by serving snacks; we showed love because we owed a "debt.")

◆ **Why does God tell us to "owe" love to each other?** (So we'll understand that we should always love each other; to remind us of the importance of loving others.)

◆ **How could following the instructions of Romans 13:8-10 make you a "gold medal" friend?** (It could help me act unselfishly toward my friends; it could remind me to treat my friends the way I want to be treated.)

◆ **What can you do this week to follow the instructions of Romans 13:8-10 in the way you treat your friends?** (I can be more encouraging to my friends; I can avoid putting down my friends; I can look for ways to help out my friends.)

Say: **The advice of Romans 13:8-10 gives a solid base for building gold medal friendships because** we make **friends by caring about others. Let's explore this idea more.**

TEACHER TIP

Encourage active participation as students report back by following up kids' answers with questions such as "What did you mean by that?" and "Can you tell me more?"

THE **POINT**

GOOD FRIENDS, GOOD DEEDS

(8 to 13 minutes)

Say: **Being a gold medal friend isn't easy. Let's listen to a _cassette_ segment about a friend in a tough situation.**

Play "Good Friends, Good Deeds" from the _cassette._

Pause the tape when the narrator instructs you to do so. Have the kids form groups of no more than three to discuss the following questions:

◆ **How do you think Jenny feels right now?** (I think she wants to keep her friend; I don't think she wants to cheat; maybe she's mad at Nikki.)

◆ **When have you felt like Jenny feels?** (When my older sister wanted me to lie to my parents about what time she got home; when my friends shoplifted candy and stuff from the store.)

◆ **If Jenny is really Nikki's friend, what will she do? Explain.** (Nikki is not much of a friend if she asks Jenny to do something wrong; Jenny should find some other way to help Nikki.)

Have one person in each trio read **Hebrews 10:24** aloud. Then have the other two trio members summarize the verse in one sentence. Ask:

◆ **Based on this verse, what kind of advice would you give Jenny?** (She shouldn't cheat; she should encourage Nikki to do the right thing.)

◆ **How can you be a caring friend when a friend asks you to do something you know is wrong?** (You can suggest a different activity instead; you can explain why you think it's wrong.)

◆ **Suppose your friend becomes angry and wants to end the friendship because you try to do the right thing. What should you do?** (Continue to act in a friendly way, even when she's mean to me; be willing to lose a friend, if necessary; try to include him in other activities so he'll know I still want to be his friend.)

◆ **What makes it hard to live out the instructions of Hebrews 10:24 with your friends?** (I'm afraid they'll stop being my friends; I don't want to disappoint my friends.)

◆ **What are other ways you can follow the instructions in this verse this week?** (Don't ask my friends to do something I know is wrong; encourage my friends to do the right thing, like obeying their parents.)

Say: **In your groups, think of a way that Jenny could answer Nikki and still be her friend. Be ready to report back to the group in two minutes.**

Give a sheet of paper and a pencil to each group. In two minutes, sound the *squeaker* to draw the groups back together. When everyone responds by raising their hands and focusing on you, have representatives from the groups report their ideas.

Then say: **Let's find out how this story ends.**

Play the rest of the "Good Friends, Good Deeds" segment.

After the end of the story, turn off the *cassette* and save it for future lessons.

Say: **We make friends by caring about others. Even though she had to risk making Nikki mad, Jenny showed she cared by refusing to help Nikki do something she knew was wrong. Although it may be hard at times, we can show our friends the same type of caring attitude that Jenny showed Nikki.**

🔊 THE **POINT**

PHONY ENCOURAGEMENT

LEARNING LAB

(7 to 12 minutes)

On 3×5 cards before class, write ridiculously phony compliments such as these:
- ◆ "You are the most beautiful girl in the world."
- ◆ "Einstein couldn't be any smarter than you are."
- ◆ "You are the best basketball player I have ever seen."
- ◆ "I've never seen a guy who's as strong as you are."
- ◆ "Your skin is as soft as rose petals."
- ◆ "Thinking of you makes me deliriously happy."

Add your own outrageous compliments as well. Begin this activity by saying: **Let's do another activity to help us explore more about being gold medal friends**.

Give one of your phony-compliment cards to each student (it's OK to give the same compliment card to more than one student). Tell kids they've got 30 seconds to give the compliments on their cards to as many people as possible. Kids can't vary the compliment at all, even if it's totally inappropriate (for example, telling a boy he's "the most beautiful girl in the world").

After 30 seconds, sound the *squeaker* to regain kids' attention. When kids respond by raising their hands and focusing on you, ask:

◆ **What did you think about giving and getting these compliments? Explain.** (I thought it was silly because the compliments were fake; I thought it was funny because we said crazy things.)

◆ **How would you like it if these kinds of compliments**

were the only encouragement you got from your friends? (I'd like it because it's always fun to hear that I'm great; I'd hate it because I'd know they weren't being honest.)

◆ How can giving sincere encouragement communicate that you are a caring friend? (It tells others that I appreciate good things about them; it tells others that I want them to succeed.)

Say: Phony encouragement doesn't help us make friends because it's not sincere. We need to learn how to give encouragement that shows our friends we care. Let's look in the Bible for a hint about how to do this.

Have kids choose a friend they feel comfortable having for a discussion partner. Then have one partner in each pair read Philippians 4:8 and the other summarize it. Next have pairs discuss these questions:

◆ What would a thoughtful compliment or act of encouragement have to be like to reflect Philippians 4:8? (It would have to be real; it would have to focus on the positive qualities listed in this verse.)

◆ When would it be appropriate to encourage a friend with a compliment or action based in Philippians 4:8? (Any time; when a friend feels discouraged; when a friend succeeds at something.)

◆ What can you do this week to thoughtfully encourage a friend? (Think about what I like about my friends, then tell them; give a sincere compliment to someone each day.)

Sound the *squeaker* to end the discussions. When kids respond by raising their hands and focusing on you, have pairs take turns reporting any new insights they gained.

Say: We practiced insincere encouragement earlier. Now let's practice sincere encouragement. Think about your partner's positive qualities for a minute. Then complete this sentence with him or her in mind but don't say it out loud yet. The sentence is "You deserve a gold medal friendship award because . . ."

For example, you might complete the sentence with "you're a person who really likes to help others," "you have a real talent for making people feel comfortable," or "I've noticed that you love your little sister a lot." Remember, don't say it out loud!

Give kids a minute of "think time." Then have pairs divide themselves into ones and twos. Have all the ones form a line in front of the class.

Next, give the *gold medallions* to the twos for a mock awards ceremony. Have the twos take turns telling their partners how they completed the sentence and hanging the *gold medallions* on their partners' necks. Then have partners switch places while the ones repeat the process for the twos.

Afterward, say: 👉 **We make friends by caring about others. Giving sincere encouragement is a terrific way to express that we care. Plan on doing that this week at home, school, or anywhere.**

TABLE™ TENT

We believe Christian education extends beyond the classroom into the home. Photocopy the "Table Tent" handout (p. 122) for this week and send it home with your kids. Encourage kids and parents to use the handout to spark meaningful discussion on this week's topic. Follow up next week by asking kids how their discussions went with their families.

CLOSING

THE GOLDEN RULE

(5 to 10 minutes)

Form a circle and have kids give the answer to the following question in unison:

◆ **What was The Point of today's lesson?** (We make friends by caring about others.)

Give everyone a 3×5 card and a pencil. On their cards, have kids write one sentence describing how someone showed friendship in a caring, meaningful way to them.

For example, kids might write "My friend helped me with my math homework when I didn't understand it," "My friend gave me a gift for no reason," or "My brother visited me in the hospital when I had my tonsils out."

Have kids stack their cards face down in the upturned *mini straw hat.*

Say: 👉 **We make friends by caring about others. If you're ever unsure about how to show that you care, remember what Jesus said in Matthew 7:12: "Do to others what you want them to do to you." This is the golden rule for gold medal friendships.**

Shuffle the 3×5 cards and return them to the hat. Pass the hat around the circle and have kids each draw a card.

LEARNING LAB

Say: **On our cards we've written ways we like our friends to treat us. Read your card now, then pray silently. Ask God to help you use the situation on your card this week to give you a new idea for showing a friend that you care.**

Give kids a moment to pray, then close the prayer time by asking God to help your students make friends by caring about others. Retrieve the *mini straw hat* for use in later lessons.

DEBT CARDS

Photocopy and cut apart these cards for use in the "Tongue Twister Debts" activity. Fold the cards so that only the words "Debt Card" are visible. Make sure you have at least one card for each student in your class.

DEBT CARD	"Always owe love to each other" (Romans 13:8b).	Show love to a classmate by serving a snack to someone who hasn't had one yet.
DEBT CARD	"Always owe love to each other" (Romans 13:8b).	Show love to a classmate by serving a snack to someone who hasn't had one yet.
DEBT CARD	"Always owe love to each other" (Romans 13:8b).	Show love to a classmate by serving a snack to someone who hasn't had one yet.
DEBT CARD	"Always owe love to each other" (Romans 13:8b).	Show love to a classmate by serving a snack to someone who hasn't had one yet.

Rachel was disappointed to discover that caring for friends included weeding the garden.

"Always owe love to each other" (Romans 13:8b).

Talk Triggers

▲ Who are your best friends? Why are they your best friends?

▲ Why is it sometimes hard to care for others? When should your own needs come first?

THE WORD on Success in Friendships

Monday   John 13:34-35
Why is it important for friends to love each other?

Tuesday   John 13:13-15
How can you follow Jesus' example of caring for others?

Wednesday   Proverbs 17:17
What's difficult about living by the standards of this verse? How can you overcome those difficulties?

Thursday   Proverbs 18:24
How can you demonstrate loyalty in your friendships?

Friday   John 3:16
How did God show that he cares for us? What should our response be?

Saturday   John 15:13-15
In what ways can you be a "gold medal" friend to Jesus?

THE AGONY OF DEFEAT

THE POINT

☞ **God can make our failures stepping stones to success.**

THE BIBLE BASIS

Luke 22:54-62

They arrested Jesus, and led him away, and brought him into the house of the high priest. Peter followed far behind them. After the soldiers started a fire in the middle of the courtyard and sat together, Peter sat with them. A servant girl saw Peter sitting there in the firelight, and looking closely at him, she said, "This man was also with him."

But Peter said this was not true; he said, "Woman, I don't know him."

A short time later, another person saw Peter and said, "You are also one of them."

But Peter said, "Man, I am not!"

About an hour later, another man insisted, "Certainly this man was with him, because he is from Galilee, too."

But Peter said, "Man, I don't know what you are talking about!"

At once, while Peter was still speaking, a rooster crowed. Then the Lord turned and looked straight at Peter. And Peter remembered what the Lord had said: "Before the rooster crows this day, you will say three times that you don't know me." Then Peter went outside and cried painfully.

Hours before Jesus' arrest, Peter boldly declared, "Lord (Jesus), I am ready... even to die with you!" (Luke 22:33). But Peter's boldness in private became cowardice in public. The accusation of a servant girl was all it took for Peter to deny any knowledge of Jesus. That Peter failed in the face of opposition is tragic. That Peter refused to be beaten by failure is glorious.

History records that Peter moved beyond his failure to become one of the most influential members of the early church. He ended his life as a martyr, unwilling to deny his Lord again.

Like Peter, fifth- and sixth-graders know what it's like to fail. Falling short of parents' expectations, inability to break into the popular crowd, getting picked last when teams are chosen—all of these situations lead kids to brand themselves as failures.

Kids need help to see beyond the disappointments of their present experience. Use this lesson to show your kids how God can take today's failures and turn them into tomorrow's successes. Other Scriptures used in the lesson are **1 Kings 19:4-18** and **Colossians 3:12-14.**

GETTING THE POINT ━━━━━━

Students will
◆ examine the story of Peter's denial;
◆ be encouraged not to give up too easily; and
◆ discover how, with God's help, they can help each other overcome failures.

THIS LESSON AT A GLANCE

SECTION	MINUTES	WHAT STUDENTS WILL DO	LEARNING LAB SUPPLIES	CLASSROOM SUPPLIES
ATTENTION GRABBER	5 to 10	**Stone Toss**—Experience failure in a game.	Checked mat, scented stones	3×5 cards, marker, masking tape
BIBLE EXPLORATION AND APPLICATION	7 to 12	**Speak Up**—Interview each other on the topic of failure and discuss Peter's failure in Luke 22:54-62.	Cassette: "Speak-Up Interviews"	Bibles, cassette player, newsprint, marker, paper, pencils
	8 to 13	**Give Up?**—Examine the story of Elijah in 1 Kings 19:4-18 after advising "clients" not to give up.		Bibles, "Give Up?" hand-out (p. 134), pencils, paper
	10 to 15	**Fuzzy Friends**—Help each other over-come possible failure and talk about Colossians 3:12-14.	Fuzzy fleece, elastic strips	Bibles, newsprint, marker
CLOSING	5 to 10	**Humble Reflections**—Learn a new song about humility and share about a time when God turned a humbling experience into a success.	Cassette: "Humble Thyself in the Sight of the Lord," lyrics poster	Cassette player

Remember to make photocopies of the "Table Tent" handout (p. 135) to send home with your kids. The "Table Tent" is a valuable tool for helping fifth- and sixth-graders talk with their parents about what they're learning in class.

THE LESSON

> Before the lesson, collect the necessary items from the Learning Lab for the activities you plan to use. Refer to the pictures in the margins to see what each item looks like.
>
> As kids arrive, ask them about last week's "Table Tent" discussion. Use questions such as "What did you learn about your family?" and "What surprised you about your family's reactions?" However, be careful not to embarrass students whose families choose not to use the "Table Tent."

ATTENTION GRABBER

STONE TOSS

(5 to 10 minutes)

Begin class with a reminder to kids that whenever you sound the *squeaker,* they're to stop what they're doing, raise their hands, and focus on you. Practice the signal two or three times.

Write the following words on separate 3×5 cards: "awesome," "perfect," "winner," and "star."

Tape the 3×5 cards to different areas on the *checked mat* and place the mat on the floor. Make a line with masking tape on the floor about 10 feet away from the mat, then have kids form a line behind the tape. Designate a "loser's corner" in the room. Then show kids the five *scented stones.*

Say: **The object of this game is to toss all five *scented stones* onto the 3×5 cards on the mat. If your stones land anywhere else on or off the mat, you fail and must go sit in the loser's corner. If you don't fail, you can play again. You must toss all your stones at once—not one at a time. Ready? I'll go first.**

Begin the game. After you've banished yourself to the loser's corner, have the other kids in line take turns tossing the stones. Welcome kids into your corner with encouraging words after they fail. If someone does get all five stones on the 3×5 cards, applaud him or her and have that person go again. It's highly unlikely that anyone will succeed once and practically impossible to succeed twice in a row.

After everyone is gathered in the loser's corner, form groups of no more than three. Direct students to number off within their trios from one to three.

Say: **Discuss the next few questions in your trio. Then I'll call out a number between one and three. The person**

LEARNING LAB

TEACHER TIP

If you have 10 or more students in class, you may want to have them form two lines to speed up the activity.

Also, it's important that you be the first player in the game and that you maintain a good attitude about being sent to the loser's corner. That'll make it easier for other kids to experience "failing" in the game.

in your group whose number I call out will be responsible for sharing your answer. Here's my first question:

◆ **What went through your mind when you failed at this game?** (I was bummed because I failed in front of everybody; I was disappointed because I really thought I could do it; I was OK because everybody else failed, too.)

◆ **How does it make you feel when you fail to be awesome, perfect, or a star in real life? Explain.** (Like a loser because I don't measure up; disappointed because I try hard.)

◆ **When does failure make you feel like you've been stuck in a loser's corner?** (When I keep getting poor grades even though I study; when others depend on me and I let them down; when I think that there's nothing I'm very good at.)

Say: **We all fail at one time or another, but that's OK. ✍ God can make our failures stepping stones to success. Today we're going to learn more about what that means.**

✍ THE **POINT**

BIBLE EXPLORATION AND APPLICATION

SPEAK UP

(7 to 12 minutes)

Write the following interview questions on newsprint:
◆ How would you define failure?
◆ What kinds of failures have you experienced?
◆ How do you think God views failure?

Form two teams—a team of "experts" and a team of "reporters." Distribute paper and pencils to the reporters, then say: **Reporters, you work for the Daily Gazette newspaper. Your first assignment is to interview an expert to discover his or her answers to the questions on this newsprint. Write the results of your interviews on your papers and be ready to report your discoveries to the class.**

Experts, you work for the National Institute of Failure Research. Your job is to answer the questions on this newsprint for your reporters. You've got two minutes to be interviewed. Ready? Go!

Have kids spend two minutes in the interviews, then tell

LEARNING LAB

kids to switch roles. After everyone has been interviewed, sound the *squeaker* to regain students' attention and wait for kids to respond. Invite kids to report discoveries they gained from their interviews.

Then say: **Let's listen to what other kids your age have to say on the topic of failure.**

Play "Speak-Up Interviews" from the *cassette*.

When the segment is finished, ask:

◆ **How did the ideas you came up with in your interviews compare to what you heard on the *cassette*?** (We had different definitions of failure; the kids on the *cassette* have experienced the same kinds of failures we have.)

◆ **Why do you think God allows everyone to experience failure?** (So we can grow from it; so we'll realize we need to depend on God.)

Say: **Peter, one of Jesus' disciples, experienced a failure that must have made him feel like a loser. Luke 22:33 records that before Jesus was arrested, Peter said, "Lord, I am ready to go with you to prison and even to die with you!" In your groups, read Luke 22:54-62 to find out what Peter really did.**

Have pairs read the story. Then have kids discuss these questions:

◆ **Why do you think Peter failed to stand up for Jesus?** (He was scared; he didn't expect to be challenged; he wasn't as prepared as he thought.)

◆ **What do you think Peter should have done after realizing he failed?** (Talked to a friend about it; prayed about it; figured out why he failed; tried again.)

◆ **How do the failures you experience compare to Peter's failure in this passage?** (Peter felt pressure and so do I; Peter must have felt terrible afterward, but it doesn't really bother me to fail.)

◆ **In what ways are you like Peter?** (I sometimes fail to stand up for Jesus; I sometimes brag too much; I want to do well, but sometimes pressure gets to me.)

◆ **What's one thing you can learn from Peter's failure to help you face failure this week?** (I shouldn't be afraid to stand up for Jesus; I shouldn't brag; I should remain calm under pressure.)

Say: **Because of his disappointing failure, Peter could have given up and walked away from God, but he didn't. After Jesus' resurrection, God used Peter to become one of the main leaders in the early church. Peter's story is just another example that shows**  **God can make our failures stepping stones to success.**

THE **POINT**

GIVE UP?

(8 to 13 minutes)

Have kids find new partners to form groups of no more than four. Tell groups to assign the following roles within their foursomes: a recorder who writes down the group's thoughts; a representative who shares the group's thoughts with the class; a reader who'll read the client profiles and the Scriptures; and an encourager who urges everyone to participate in the discussion.

Say: **Your group is now a talent agency. In a moment, I'll give the readers in each group a profile of one of your clients. Your responsibility as a talent agency is to talk your client out of giving up on his or her goals. Think of what you might say to your client and write it down. Your representative will present your ideas to the class in four minutes. Ready? Let's go.**

Give each group's reader a client profile. After four minutes, sound the *squeaker* to regain kids' attention. When everyone has responded by raising their hands and focusing on you, have representatives briefly describe their clients' profiles and the ideas their groups came up with.

Afterward, say: **Your clients are real people. Client #1 was Babe Ruth, the greatest baseball player of his time. Although he struck out 1,330 times, he hit a record 714 home runs in his career. Client #2 was English novelist John Creasey. After getting 753 rejection slips, he went on to publish 564 books. Client #3 is R. H. Macy, founder of the Macy's department store chain, based in New York City.**

And Client #4 is you. As a baby you were unable to walk and often fell. But you didn't give up, and now walking is something you don't even think about.

Ask these questions one at a time, pausing for group discussion after each one:

◆ **What was easy or difficult for you during this activity?** (It was hard to think of reasons for someone who had struck out over 1,000 times to keep trying; it was easy to think of ways to encourage someone to walk.)

◆ **What surprised you most about this activity?** (That someone could get 753 rejections slips and still be a successful writer; that I was client #4.)

◆ **What do you think your clients might have learned from their failures that could've helped them succeed later?** (How not to do something; the importance of not giving up.)

> ## TEACHER TIP
>
> Be sure to provide a pencil and a sheet of paper for each group's recorder.

Sound the *squeaker* to end group discussions. After kids respond by raising their hands and focusing on you, invite representatives to share any insights their groups gained as they answered the questions.

Say: **The prophet Elijah experienced a failure that made him feel like giving up. Elijah won a battle with the false prophets of Baal, and he hoped that people would serve God because of it. Instead, it just made Queen Jezebel furious. She gave orders for Elijah to be killed. Elijah ran away into the desert to hide. In your groups, read 1 Kings 19:4-18 to see what happened next.**

Give kids a couple of minutes to read the Bible passage. Then ask:

◆ **How did Elijah respond to failure?** (He ran away; he wanted to give up.)

◆ **If Elijah had been one of your clients, what would you have said to him?** (Hang in there, God still cares about you; it seems tough now, but you can trust God to help you.)

◆ **How did God respond to Elijah's failure?** (God sent an angel to strengthen Elijah; God encouraged Elijah; God gave Elijah a plan for success.)

◆ **What can you learn about failure from this activity and from the story of Elijah to help you this week?** (It's important not to give up; God can make our failures stepping stones to success.)

Say: **Like Elijah and our clients, we don't have to be trapped by failure because** ☞ **God can make our failures stepping stones to success. Remember that when you encounter failures this week.**

THE POINT ☞

LEARNING LAB

FUZZY FRIENDS

(10 to 15 minutes)

Say: **Sometimes God uses us to help each other overcome failure. Let's play a game to show what I mean.**

Form a circle and place one volunteer in the center. Show kids the *fuzzy fleece* and the *elastic strips.*

Say: **The object of this game is to see how many times our volunteer can catch the *fuzzy fleece* while blindfolded with the *elastic strips*. Without our help, our volunteer will probably fail. But we're going to help** (volunteer's name).

I'll throw the *fuzzy fleece* into the air toward the volunteer. When it reaches the height of its arc, we'll all shout "Now!" and that'll be the clue for the volunteer to reach out to catch the fleece. If we do our job right, our

volunteer should be able to catch the fleece just from hearing our cue. Ready? Let's try it!

Tie the *elastic strips* loosely over the volunteer's eyes to blindfold him or her. Then toss the *fuzzy fleece* gently into the air so that it'll come down right in front of the volunteer. When the fleece reaches the highest point of its arc, signal the kids to shout "Now!" for the volunteer. Give the volunteer three chances, then ask for a new volunteer. Repeat with as many volunteers as time allows.

End the game after five minutes or after everyone has had an opportunity to be the volunteer. Retrieve the *fuzzy fleece* and *elastic strips* for later use.

Form pairs for discussion and have partners discuss the following questions one at a time. Write them on newsprint for kids to refer to during discussions. Ask:

◆ **How did it feel to help each other succeed at this game? Explain.** (It was exciting because it really worked; I was surprised to see how many times the volunteers caught the fleece.)

◆ **How can we help each other succeed in real life?** (By encouraging each other; by praying for each other; by rooting for each other to do well.)

◆ **Why is it important to have friends and family members who encourage us when we fail?** (So we don't get too depressed by failing; because friends and family members can encourage us to try again.)

Sound the *squeaker* to pause discussions. When kids have raised their hands and focused on you, invite pairs to share their insights. Then have one partner in each pair read **Colossians 3:12-14** and the other summarize it in one sentence. Ask:

◆ **How could following the instructions of Colossians 3:12-14 help others to succeed?** (Being patient can encourage others to try again even though they've failed once; forgiving can help us overcome hurt feelings when others let us down.)

◆ **Why do you think God wants us to encourage each other in this way?** (Because Christians ought to be able to depend on other Christians; because then we'll help each other get past our failures.)

◆ **When has a friend or family member encouraged you in a way described by Colossians 3:12-14? Explain.** (My mom always gives me a second chance when I make a mistake; my friend is always kind and encourages me to do better.)

◆ **What can you do this week to help friends or family members overcome feelings of failure?** (I can encourage them to keep trying; I can remind them of their past successes; I can tell them that God can make their failures stepping stones to success.)

Sound the *squeaker* to end discussions and wait for kids to respond. Invite volunteers to tell any interesting answers they talked about.

Then say: ☞**God can make our failures stepping stones to success. By encouraging and helping each other, we can become God's agents to help turn failures into successes. Let's practice encouraging each other right now.**

Re-form the circle and place the *fuzzy fleece* in the center. Have a volunteer stand on the fleece. Tell kids they have five seconds to think of one positive word of encouragement to describe that person. For example, kids might think of words like "awesome," "friendly," or "smart."

Next, on the count of three, have kids call out their descriptive words at the same time. Repeat the process with new volunteers until everyone has had a chance to stand on the *fuzzy fleece.* Then retrieve the fleece and move on to the closing.

THE **POINT** ☞

TABLE™ TENT

We believe Christian education extends beyond the classroom into the home. Photocopy the "Table Tent" handout (p. 135) for this week and send it home with your kids. Encourage kids and parents to use the handout to spark meaningful discussion on this week's topic. Follow up next week by asking kids how their discussions went with their families.

LEARNING LAB

THE **POINT** ☞

CLOSING

HUMBLE REFLECTIONS

(5 to 10 minutes)

Say: **Let's learn a song to help us remember that** ☞**God can make our failures stepping stones to success. Sing this song during the week to remind you that God helps us grow and learn from our failures.**

Teach kids "Humble Thyself in the Sight of the Lord." Use

the *cassette* and the *lyrics poster* to assist you. Afterward invite kids to take turns answering these questions:

◆ **Why do you think God likes to turn mistakes and failures into growing experiences?** (Because God cares about us; because it helps us rely on God.)

◆ **When was a time God turned one of your humbling experiences into a successful one?** (I lost a basketball game, but I ended up becoming friends with a guy from the other team; I failed a math test once, and it made me want to study and do well on the next one.)

After kids have shared their answers, have everyone form a huddle and make a pile of hands in the center. Then, to dismiss, have kids shout out in unison the answer to the following question: **What was The Point of today's lesson?** (God can make our failures stepping stones to success.)

TEACHER TIP

Before having kids answer the second question, you may want to set the tone by sharing a failure that grew into a success in your own life.

Give Up?

Photocopy and cut apart the client profiles below for use in the "Give Up?" activity during the lesson. You'll need at least one profile for every four students.

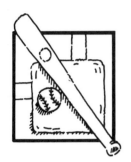

Client #1

Your client wants to be the best professional baseball player of his time. He's just got one problem: hitting the ball. He has a decent swing with plenty of power, but he has trouble connecting with the ball. As a matter of fact, he's struck out 1,330 times in his career. Your client feels like giving up. What can you say to keep him from quitting?

Client #2

Your client wants to be a successful writer of novels. He's written quite a few things, but no one seems interested. As a matter of fact, he's just received his 753rd rejection slip. Your client feels like giving up. What can you say to keep him from quitting?

Client #3

Your client wants to start a world-famous department store. He's got good ideas but a poor track record. As a matter of fact, he's tried seven times to start his store and failed every time. Your client feels like giving up. What can you say to keep him from quitting?

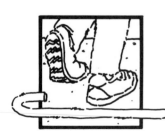

Client #4

Your client is hampered by a mental and physical disability that makes this person unable to walk. Your client has tried many times to walk but always falls down, sometimes causing injury. Your client feels like giving up. What can you say to keep your client from quitting?

TABLE™ TENT

"They arrested Jesus, and led him away, and brought him into the house of the high priest. Peter followed far behind them" (Luke 22:54).

Talk Triggers

◆ What makes you feel like a success or failure as a Christian?

◆ Describe a time God turned one of your failures into a stepping stone for success.

THE WORD on Failure and Disappointment

Monday   Proverbs 16:1
In what ways do you need God's help going from one stepping stone to another in life?

Tuesday   1 Peter 1:3-8
How can the promises in this passage give you hope in the face of failure?

Wednesday   Psalm 51:1-12
When has failure made you feel like the author of this psalm? What did you do about it?

Thursday   Romans 8:28
What current failures could God be using right now as "stepping stones" to bring out good in the long run?

Friday   Proverbs 16:3
How does depending on God help you to deal with failure?

Saturday   Luke 23:32-43
Why do you think Jesus had to experience the crucifixion, which looked like a failure to his friends and his enemies both? How did God use Jesus' death as a stepping stone to eternal success?

(fold here)

Success and Failure, Week 11

REACHING FOR HEAVEN

THE POINT

☞ **True success is becoming like Jesus.**

THE BIBLE BASIS

Philippians 1:20

> I expect and hope that I will not fail Christ in anything but that I will have the courage now, as always, to show the greatness of Christ in my life here on earth, whether I live or die.

When Paul says in Philippians 1:20, "whether I live or die," it's not merely a poetic phrase. As he wrote this letter, he was being held prisoner in Rome, awaiting trial before Caesar—a trial that could result in his death. With the clarity of thought of a man whose days are numbered, he tells the Philippians of his greatest success: "to show the greatness of Christ in my life."

Fifth- and sixth-graders are developing ideas about success from parents, school, church, television, and other popular entertainment. They often think that success is equivalent to fame, wealth, or ability. Kids need to discover what Paul knew—that becoming like Jesus is the key to true success. Use this lesson to help kids understand God's measure of success.

Other Scriptures used in this lesson are **Matthew 4:1-11; 7:24-29; 18:1-4, 21-22; 19:26; Philippians 2:5-11, 13; 4:19; Luke 1:37; Isaiah 40:29, 31;** and **2 Corinthians 12:9.**

GETTING THE POINT

Students will
◆ explore qualities of Jesus they can imitate,
◆ discover the importance of serving others like Jesus did, and
◆ learn how to be like Jesus.

THIS LESSON AT A GLANCE

SECTION	MINUTES	WHAT STUDENTS WILL DO	LEARNING LAB SUPPLIES	CLASSROOM SUPPLIES
ATTENTION GRABBER	5 to 10	**Flipper Success**—Play an elimination game to define success.	Elastic strips, flippers	
BIBLE EXPLORATION AND APPLICATION	10 to 15	**TV Guides**—Write TV Guide entries for new shows that reflect various Scriptures.		Bibles, 3×5 cards, paper, pencils, newsprint
	8 to 13	**Steps to Success**—Help each other succeed, then discuss Philippians 1:20 and 2:5-11.	Mini straw hat	Bibles, paper, pencils, masking tape, 3×5 cards
	7 to 12	**Power to be Perfect**—Compare being perfect in an activity to becoming like Jesus, then be encouraged by several Scriptures about God's power.	Carpenter wreath, elastic strip, flipper, plastic bat, squeeze ball	Bibles, masking tape
CLOSING	5 to 10	**Heads or Tails?**—Encourage each other as they become more like Jesus each day.	Gold medallion	Marker

Remember to make photocopies of the "Table Tent" handout (p. 147) to send home with your kids. The "Table Tent" is a valuable tool for helping fifth- and sixth-graders talk with their parents about what they're learning in class.

THE LESSON

Before the lesson, collect the necessary items from the Learning Lab for the activities you plan to use. Refer to the pictures in the margins to see what each item looks like.

As kids arrive, ask them about last week's "Table Tent" discussion. Use questions such as "What did you learn about your family?" and "What surprised you about your family's reactions?" However, be careful not to embarrass students whose families choose not to use the "Table Tent."

ATTENTION GRABBER

FLIPPER SUCCESS

(5 to 10 minutes)

Begin class with a reminder that whenever you sound the *squeaker,* kids are to stop what they're doing, raise their hands, and focus on you. Practice the signal two or three times.

Tie the *elastic strips* to the legs of two chairs so that the *elastic strips* are stretched out about six inches off the floor. Give each student one *flipper,* then form a line of students behind each *elastic strip.*

Say: **Today we're going to talk about success and what it means. To start, let's do a fun exercise called "Flipper Success."**

The object of this exercise is to successfully get your *flipper* over the *elastic strip* by flipping it from the floor. You'll have only one try each round. If your try is successful, you can go to the back of your line and participate in the next round. If your try isn't successful, stand to the side and cheer for your classmates. It's all right for people from both lines to flip at the same time. Ready? Go.

After everyone has had a turn, raise the *elastic strip* a few inches for the next round. Continue raising the *elastic strip* after each round until all but one person have been eliminated. Raise that last person's hand like a boxing champ and say: **The winner and new *flipper* success... (student's name)! Hurray!**

Encourage everyone to cheer and congratulate the winner. Collect the *elastic strip* and *flippers* for later use. Ask:

◆ **How did playing this game make you feel? Explain.** (Embarrassed, because I couldn't even get one *flipper* to go

LEARNING LAB

TEACHER TIP

If you have more than 20 students, have kids take turns using the *flippers* for this activity.

THE **POINT**

over; happy, because I did really well; nervous, because I had to keep playing while everyone watched me.)

◆ **How did we define success in this game?** (Being able to flip your *flipper* over the *elastic strip;* being the last person still in the game.)

◆ **How do people define success in real life?** (Being the best at something; having a lot of money; being famous.)

◆ **How do those definitions of success influence the way people feel about the things they do?** (Some people aren't happy unless they have a lot of money; some people get discouraged when they aren't the best at something.)

Say: **People define success in many different ways, but the Bible teaches that** **true success is becoming like Jesus. Today we'll explore more about how to become true successes.**

BIBLE EXPLORATION AND APPLICATION

TV GUIDES

(10 to 15 minutes)

Write the following Scripture references on separate 3×5 cards: **Matthew 4:1-11; Matthew 7:24-29; Matthew 18:1-4; and Matthew 18:21-22.**

Say: **Because** **true success is becoming like Jesus, we need to get to know Jesus better. Let's do a fun activity to help us learn more about Jesus right now.**

Form four "executive councils" (an executive council is a group of at least two people) and give each council one of the Scripture references. Also, distribute paper and pencils to everyone.

Say: **Your group has just become an executive council for the Bible Channel. As network executives, your job is to write an exciting TV Guide entry for a new show that tells how to be like Jesus in our world today.**

You'll have to make up a show to write about, and your show should be based on the theme of your Scripture. Your show can be one of the following types: a soap opera, a situation comedy, an action show, a game show, or a talk show.

For example, you might write an entry about a soap

THE **POINT**

opera that tells how members of one family struggle to forgive each other. Or you might write an entry about a game show where you win valuable prizes by bragging about others instead of yourself. Be creative and have fun with this. Make sure everyone in your council has a copy of your TV Guide entry. You've got five minutes to prepare. Go!

After five minutes, sound the *squeaker* to regain kids' attention. When kids respond by raising their hands and focusing on you, have them choose a new partner from each of the other three councils to form new groups of no more than four.

In their new groups, have kids take turns reading aloud the Scriptures assigned to their executive councils, and their TV Guide entries. Afterward, have foursomes discuss these questions. Write the questions on newsprint for kids to refer to during discussions. Ask:

◆ **Why do people work so hard to imitate their heroes?** (Because they think their heroes are great; because they want to be successful like their heroes are.)

◆ **What does it mean when we say we want to be like Jesus?** (That Jesus is our hero; that we're not ashamed of our faith in God.)

◆ **Why should we be like Jesus? Why not Paul or Moses or someone else?** (Because Jesus is God; because Jesus is the only perfect person; because Moses and Paul failed at times, but Jesus never fails.)

◆ **What did you learn from this activity that can help you be like Jesus?** (Jesus relied on God's Word, and so can I; I need to obey God like Jesus commanded; Jesus cares about humble people, so I should be humble; I should forgive others because Jesus wants us to forgive.)

◆ **How would our class be different if we all tried to imitate Jesus every minute of every day?** (We'd be kinder to each other; we'd be happier with ourselves.)

◆ **What's one specific way you can imitate Jesus this week?** (I can stop putting down my friends; I can forgive my brother even though he borrowed my things without asking; I can obey God by obeying my parents.)

Sound the *squeaker* to regain kids' attention. After they respond by raising their hands and focusing on you, invite group members to share new thoughts they gained from their discussions.

Then say: **Learning how to imitate Jesus in our daily lives isn't always easy. But it's always worthwhile because** 📖 **true success is becoming like Jesus.**

 THE **POINT**

LEARNING LAB

(8 to 13 minutes)

Pass out three 3×5 cards, a piece of masking tape, a sheet of paper, and a pencil to each student. On their papers, have kids list the names of three famous, successful people. Kids might write names such as Shaquille O'Neal, Amy Grant, or a local celebrity's name. Have kids tape their papers to their clothes.

Say: **The people on your list are successful for exceeding the world's standards in areas such as sports, entertainment, wealth, or ability. But Jesus set a different standard for success. Let's play a game to explore that more.**

Have kids write one name from their lists on each of their 3×5 cards, then pass their cards to you. Shuffle the 3×5 cards and place them in the *mini straw hat*. You'll draw them out of the hat during the activity.

Form two teams and have them line up against opposite walls.

Say: **This game is called "Steps to Success." The first team to have all its members touch the opposite wall wins, but you'll have to help each other move across the floor.**

Here's how it works: I'll call out a number of steps, such as "five baby steps" or "three giant steps." Then I'll draw a card from the hat. If a name I draw matches a name on your list, you can choose one of your teammates to move the appropriate number of steps. No one can move unless chosen by a teammate.

When kids understand the rules, begin the game. Here are some more ideas for steps you can use during the game: four rabbit bounces, 12 mouse-sized steps, five one-foot hops, three Goliath-sized steps, two steps backward and once step forward, or two normal-sized steps.

Lead kids in applauding the team that finishes first. Then have students each choose a partner from the opposing team to form pairs for discussion. Ask the following questions one at a time and allow kids time to briefly discuss each one with their partners.

◆ **What went through your mind as you played this game?** (I was hoping one of my cards would get drawn so I could help my team; I wanted to be sure to pick someone in back so we all could win.)

◆ **How does the winning strategy in this game compare with what you must do to be successful at most games?**

(You usually don't try to help other people; you usually just try to finish first.)

◆ **What do you think Jesus' "winning strategy" for life is?** (To love and follow God; to help others.)

Sound the *squeaker* to regain the group's attention. After kids have responded by raising their hands and focusing on you, invite pairs to share insights they gained during their discussions.

Next have partners take turns reading and summarizing **Philippians 1:20** and **2:5-11.** Ask:

◆ **How is Jesus like a helping teammate in our game?** (Jesus helped us all by dying on the cross; Jesus makes it possible for us to succeed in life; Jesus helps us to show his greatness to the world.)

◆ **In what ways is helping others succeed a winning strategy for "showing the greatness of Christ" to the world?** (It helps us become more like Jesus in our everyday lives; it helps others see Jesus in us.)

◆ **What makes it hard for you to follow Christ's example of service described in these Scriptures?** (I get caught up in serving myself instead of others; I don't know how far I should go in serving others.)

◆ **What can you do this week to overcome those obstacles?** (Play "Steps to Success" with my friends as a reminder to help others; read the Bible; plan ways to help others this week.)

Say: ✍ **True success is becoming like Jesus and following his example of service to others. Let's do our best to become successful in God's eyes by helping others this week.**

🐾 THE **POINT**

POWER TO BE PERFECT 📖

(7 to 12 minutes)

LEARNING LAB

Use an *elastic strip* to hang the *carpenter wreath* from the ceiling in the center of the room. Have kids form a single file line behind a strip of masking tape about five feet away from the wreath.

Give the first person in line the *flipper,* the *plastic bat,* and the *squeeze ball.* Say: **When I start the wreath swinging, you'll have 10 seconds to throw each of these items through the wreath. Then the next person in line will try it, and so on, until everyone has had a turn. Do your best to get all three through the wreath, if you can.**

Gently push the *carpenter wreath* to begin its swaying, then signal the kids to start throwing. Applaud any students who

THE **POINT** ☞

get a Learning Lab item through the wreath and give consoling encouragements to kids when they miss.

Afterward, gather everyone on one side of the masking tape line for the next series of questions. Have kids take turns sharing their responses to each question. When one student shares an answer, allow anyone who thought of the same answer—and has nothing more to add—to cross the line. When all students have crossed the line, ask the next question and repeat the process. Ask:

◆ **What was easy for you about this activity?** (It was easy to throw the *flipper* because it was small; the bat was easier to aim.)

◆ **Why was it hard to be perfect in this game?** (Because the wreath kept spinning; because the three items we threw were all different.)

◆ **How was trying to be perfect in this game like trying to be perfect like Jesus?** (Too many things make it hard for me to be perfect; it's too easy to make mistakes; both seem impossible.)

Assign the following verses to different kids to "pop up" and read aloud, one right after the other: **Luke 1:37; Isaiah 40:29; 2 Corinthians 12:9; Philippians 2:13; Isaiah 40:31; Philippians 4:19;** and **Matthew 19:26.**

After kids have read all the verses, ask:

◆ **What can you learn from these Scriptures and the activity to make it easier for you to be like Jesus?** (I can't do it by myself; God can make it possible for me to succeed in becoming like Jesus.)

◆ **What do you think will happen if we try to become like Jesus without getting power from God to help us?** (We'll get tired; we'll fail; we'll want to give up.)

◆ **How can you rely on God's power this week to make you like Jesus?** (Pray; ask God to help me each day; read my Bible for encouragement.)

Say: ☞**True success is becoming like Jesus, but when we try to be perfect all by ourselves, we get tired, frustrated, and are doomed to fail. It's impossible to become like Jesus by ourselves, but that's all right. We've got God to help us, and God can do anything!**

CLOSING

HEADS OR TAILS?

(5 to 10 minutes)

Remove a *gold medallion* from its chain (see diagram). Use a marker to draw a smiley face on one side and a dog's tail on the other.

Form a circle. Say: ☞**True success is becoming like Jesus, and it doesn't happen overnight. Let's take a moment now to encourage each other as we become more like Jesus each day.**

Show kids the *gold medallion* and say: **I'm going to flip this *gold medallion* in the air. If it lands with the smiley face up, think of how you might complete this sentence about the person on your right: "One thing I've seen you do in this class that's like Jesus is..." You might complete the sentence with "helping others," "encouraging your teammates," or "sharing your thoughts about God."**

If the *gold medallion* lands with the dog's tail up, pray silently for the person on your left to become more like Jesus this week. I'll flip the coin several times, so we might do these things more than once before we're done.

Flip the *gold medallion*. If it lands with the smiley face up, give kids a moment to think, then have them take turns sharing how they completed the sentence. Continue flipping the medallion until it has landed both with the smiley face up and with the dog's tail up.

LEARNING LAB

☜ THE **POINT**

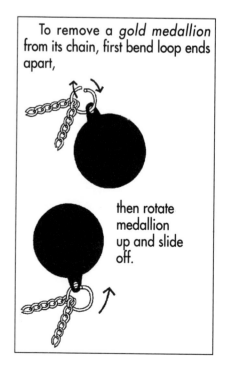

To remove a *gold medallion* from its chain, first bend loop ends apart,

then rotate medallion up and slide off.

Before dismissing class, have kids tell a partner their answers to the following question:

◆ **What will you do differently next week because of this lesson?** (Rely on God to help me become more like Jesus; help others to show Jesus to the world; read the Bible more so I can get to know Jesus better.)

THE WORD on True Success

Monday Proverbs 19:8
How can learning about God help you succeed in life?

Tuesday Colossians 2:6-7
In what ways would following the instructions in this passage make you more like Jesus?

Wednesday Psalm 119:1-2
When has this passage been true for you?

Thursday 1 John 2:1-2
How can this verse encourage you when you fail to live up to the standards set by Jesus?

Friday James 3:17
Why do you need wisdom to become like Jesus? How can you get it?

Saturday 1 Timothy 4:12-16
How can you be an example of true success?

--- (fold here) ---

"I hope that I will . . . show the greatness of Christ in my life" (Philippians 1:20b).

After reading about Jesus' temptation in Matthew 4, Nathan was worried that becoming like Jesus would mean he'd have to go without food for 40 days.

--- (fold here) ---

TALK TRIGGERS

◆ Who is one person who seems very much like Jesus to you? What do you think makes him or her that way?

◆ Why does becoming like Jesus make you a success in God's eyes?

Success and Failure, Week 12

BE-AWESOME ATTITUDES

THE POINT

☞ **God's people can be positive and joyful regardless of the circumstance.**

THE BIBLE BASIS

Philippians 1:3-6

> I thank my God for every time I remember you, always praying with joy for all of you. I thank God for the help you gave me while I preached the Good News—help you gave from the first day you believed until now. God began doing a good work in you, and I am sure he will continue it until it is finished when Jesus Christ comes again.

You'd expect Paul's letter to the Philippians to be filled with sadness, discouragement, and even a hint of bitterness. After all, he penned these words from a prison cell. Yet **Philippians 1:3-6** reveals a joyful, thankful Paul who speaks confidently of a positive future for his hearers. Paul's faith in God enabled him to maintain a positive, joyful attitude in spite of his grim circumstances.

Fifth- and sixth-graders sometimes feel as if they're in a prison cell, too. Things like peer pressure, parental expectations, failures, disappointment, loneliness, school, and everyday worries make them feel trapped by life's circumstances. But no one except kids themselves can put their attitudes in a cage. Use this lesson to help kids learn that God can help them live like Paul, with a positive and joyful outlook on life.

Other Scriptures used in the lesson are **Philippians 4:8-13** and **1 Samuel 17:22-24, 32-37, 40-50.**

GETTING THE POINT

Students will
◆ examine the effects of a negative attitude,
◆ discover how positive and joyful attitudes can help them enjoy what they do, and
◆ be encouraged to maintain a positive and joyful attitude even when others don't.

THIS LESSON AT A GLANCE

SECTION	MINUTES	WHAT STUDENTS WILL DO	LEARNING LAB SUPPLIES	CLASSROOM SUPPLIES
ATTENTION GRABBER	5 to 10	**Attitude Check**—Describe how their attitudes change based on their circumstances.	Learning Lab with all supplies in it	
BIBLE EXPLORATION AND APPLICATION	8 to 13	**Convince Me**—Talk about Philippians 1:3-6 and 4:10-13 after trying to convince the leader to overcome a negative outlook.	Plastic bat	Bibles, "Convince Me" handout (p. 159), pencils
	9 to 14	**Bowling With an Attitude**—Experience different "attitude zones" during a bowling game, then discuss Philippians 4:8-9.	Squeeze ball, checked mat, flippers	Bibles, masking tape
	8 to 13	**The Unlikely Hero**—Listen to a story, read about David and Goliath, and talk about how to maintain a positive attitude when others are concentrating on the negative.	Cassette: "The Unlikely Hero"	Bibles, cassette player
CLOSING	2 to 7	**Warm Fuzzies**—Give each other "warm fuzzies" in recognition of positive and joyful attitudes they've seen in class.	Fuzzy fleece	Scissors
QUARTER REVIEW	3 to 8	**Reflection**—Review what they've learned over the past 13 lessons.	All Learning Lab items	

Remember to make photocopies of the "Table Tent" handout (p. 160) to send home with your kids. The "Table Tent" is a valuable tool for helping fifth- and sixth-graders talk with their parents about what they're learning in class.

THE LESSON

Before the lesson, collect the necessary items from the Learning Lab for the activities you plan to use. Refer to the pictures in the margins to see what each item looks like.

As kids arrive, ask them about last week's "Table Tent" discussion. Use questions such as "What did you learn about your family?" and "What surprised you about your family's reactions?" However, be careful not to embarrass students whose families choose not to use the "Table Tent."

ATTENTION GRABBER

ATTITUDE CHECK

(5 to 10 minutes)

Begin class with a reminder to kids that whenever you sound the *squeaker*, they're to stop what they're doing, raise their hands, and focus on you. Practice the signal two or three times.

Form a circle and say: **Let's start with an "attitude check." Rate your attitude today on a scale of 1 to 10, 1 meaning you feel like you have the worst attitude right now, and 10 meaning you feel like you have the best attitude right now.**

Avoid the temptation to define "the best" or "the worst" attitude for kids. Encourage them to make their own definitions to use for the ratings.

Have kids take turns telling their ratings and explaining why they rate themselves the way they do. Follow up kids' ratings with questions such as "What did you mean by that?" and "Can you tell me more?" That'll help everyone think through how they came up with their definitions of the best and worst attitudes.

Next, show kids the Learning Lab filled with its supplies. Invite kids to tell you which Learning Lab items they think are the most fun and why. Then say: **I'll tell you what: The person whose birthday is closest to November 10 can choose one of these items to take home after class today.**

Allow the appropriate student to choose an item. However, don't let the student take the item until after class because you'll be using all of the Learning Lab supplies later in this lesson.

After the student has chosen, say: **Time for another attitude check.**

LEARNING LAB

Have kids rate themselves as before. Then ask:

◆ **How did my giving away a Learning Lab item affect your rating in the attitude check?** (It made my rating go down; my rating got much better; my rating stayed the same.)

◆ **Why did some of our attitudes change after I gave away the Learning Lab item?** (Because we were disappointed about not getting to pick an item; because we were happy for our friend who got an item.)

◆ **How was this experience like the way circumstances in life affect our attitudes?** (When we're disappointed, our attitudes get worse; it's hard to maintain a good attitude when you've been treated unfairly; when something good happens, it's easy to feel happy about life.)

THE **POINT** ☞

Say: **Situations in life can influence our attitudes in both positive and negative ways. But** ☞ **God's people can be positive and joyful regardless of the circumstance. Today we're going to explore more about what that means.**

BIBLE EXPLORATION AND APPLICATION

LEARNING LAB

CONVINCE ME

(8 to 13 minutes)

Photocopy and cut apart the "Convince Me" handout on page 159. Fold each set of instructions and give one to each person.

Say: **I have a confession to make. I'm having a confidence problem. On your papers are instructions for how to help me regain my confidence. Silently read your instructions, then think for a minute or two about how you'll act them out.** (Pause and take the *plastic bat* out of the Learning Lab.) **OK, follow your instructions to help me overcome my confidence problem right now.**

As kids try to persuade you to balance the *plastic bat* on the palm of your hand, act as if you have no confidence in yourself. Respond to kids with comments like "I don't think I can do that," "I'm just not good at athletic-type things," "I'd feel really silly and self-conscious doing that in front of everyone," "I'm not coordinated enough," and "I've never done that before."

After some persuasion, try to balance the bat and fail. Then say things like "I knew I couldn't do it," "Now I really feel dumb," and "I shouldn't have done it."

When you're ready to move on, say: **OK, I'll try once more.** Then successfully balance the bat on your palm for two seconds.

Form groups of no more than three and have groups discuss the following questions. Tell groups to assign the following roles within their trios: a representative who reports the group's answers to the class, a reader who'll read the Scriptures, and an encourager who urges everyone to participate in the discussion. Pause after each question for discussion and reports.

◆ **What characterized the attitudes you saw during this exercise?** (Lack of confidence; frustration; determination; selfishness; encouragement; lack of trust.)

◆ **What effects did our attitudes have on our actions?** (I quit because I was frustrated with you; I didn't try too hard because I thought you might trick us; I kept trying because I was determined to get you to balance the bat.)

◆ **What effect did your attitude have on my attitude?** (It encouraged you to try; it discouraged you; it put pressure on you.)

◆ **When does a negative attitude prevent you from doing your best?** (When I get discouraged about my homework; when I'm mad at my parents; when I don't feel like reading my Bible.)

Have the readers read aloud **Philippians 1:3-6** and **4:10-13** for their groups. Then ask:

◆ **Based on these Scriptures, what would you say characterizes the attitude of the author of this letter to the Philippians?** (Joy; happiness; thankfulness; confidence; contentment.)

◆ **The Apostle Paul wrote this letter while he was a prisoner in Rome. Why do you think he could have such a positive attitude?** (Because he had confidence in God; because he knew Jesus would give him strength to face any circumstance; because he knew his friends cared about him.)

◆ **How does Paul's attitude compare to my attitude about the bat?** (Paul was confident, but you weren't; Paul was joyful, but you were discouraged.)

◆ **What can we learn from my negative example and Paul's positive example that can help us have joyful attitudes like Paul?** (We can depend on God to help us no matter what; God can show us how to be joyful in any situation; there's always something to be thankful for in life.)

In their trios, have kids take turns telling each other about a

TEACHER TIP

It's easier to balance the *plastic bat* in your palm if you put the fat end down.

TEACHER TIP

You may want to let kids know a little about Paul's prison experience by sharing these facts:

◆ As a prisoner, it wasn't uncommon for Paul to be chained, tied up, or kept in blocks. (Acts 16:23-24; 21:33; 22:24)

◆ Roman soldiers were Paul's constant guards. (Acts 23:23-24; 24:23; 28:16; Philippians 1:13)

◆ Roman soldiers commonly beat their prisoners, including Paul. (Acts 16:22; 22:24)

◆ Paul's enemies tried to murder him while he was a prisoner. (Acts 23:12-22)

◆ Paul was in prison simply for believing in Jesus. (Philippians 1:13)

◆ Paul's imprisonment could have resulted in his death. (Acts 28:16-19)

difficult situation they're facing in life right now. For example, kids might tell about a fight they've had with a family member, the death of a relative, or the need to move to a new school.

Next, have each trio brainstorm three ways to keep a positive, joyful attitude in those situations. For example, kids might say they can think of things they like about their family members, read Bible passages about heaven, or join a new club at the new school.

THE POINT 👉

Say: **Like Paul,** 👉 **God's people can be positive and joyful regardless of the circumstance in the way they approach the challenges of life. From now on, each time you see a baseball bat, let it remind you of what Philippians 4:13 says: "I can do all things through Christ, because he gives me strength."**

Return the *plastic bat* to the Learning Lab before moving to the next activity.

LEARNING LAB

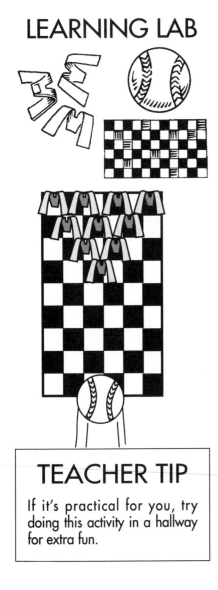

TEACHER TIP

If it's practical for you, try doing this activity in a hallway for extra fun.

BOWLING WITH AN ATTITUDE

(9 to 14 minutes)

In a corner of the room, set 10 *flippers* in bowling-pin formation at one end of the *checked mat* to create a miniature bowling alley (see diagram in margin). Have kids line up behind a strip of masking tape on the floor about five feet away from the mat.

Say: **You've just entered the "Attitude-Zone Bowling Alley." For the next two minutes, take turns "bowling" the *squeeze ball* down the alley to knock over as many *flipper* "pins" as you can. However, this alley is set up in a "bad-attitude zone." So, as you bowl, act out bad attitudes such as "selfish," "too cool for anything," "always spotting the negative aspects of a situation," and so on.**

For example, you might try to take two turns at a time instead of one, talk about how only uncool people like to bowl, or complain about how far you have to stand from the pins.

When kids understand what they're to do, give the *squeeze ball* to the first person in line and start timing. Stand near the end of the alley so you can quickly reset the pins and retrieve the ball. Watch to see how kids interact with each other during the bad-attitude time.

Sound the *squeaker* after two minutes to regain kids' attention. Wait for them to respond by raising their hands and focusing on you. Then say: **Good news! Our attitude zone has changed! We can now bowl in a "good-attitude zone."**

We'll bowl for three more minutes, but since we're in a different attitude zone, we'll have to change our actions. This time, bowlers must all cheer for each other, cooperate and share, and refuse to complain. Ready? Let's go.

Have kids take turns bowling again. Show by your example what it means to be encouraging and cooperative during the game. Sound the *squeaker* after three minutes to end the activity. When kids have responded by raising their hands and focusing on you, retrieve and put away the *squeeze ball, checked mat,* and *flippers.*

Form pairs and have partners sit together on the floor to discuss the following questions. Ask the questions one at a time, pausing for discussion after each one. Ask:

◆ **How did you feel as you bowled in the different attitude zones? Explain.** (I was frustrated in the bad-attitude zone because no one gave me a chance to bowl; I felt good bowling in the good-attitude zone because everyone encouraged me.)

◆ **How did the attitude zones affect your experience during the game? Explain.** (It was hard for me to enjoy bowling in the bad-attitude zone; I was surprised at how much more fun it was to bowl in the good-attitude zone.)

◆ **How do attitudes affect your daily life?** (When I keep a good attitude, I'm able to enjoy life more; bad attitudes make me feel like giving up.)

◆ **Why do you think attitudes make a difference in the way we experience things?** (Because a good attitude helps us see the bright side of things; because a bad attitude makes small problems seem like big ones.)

Sound the *squeaker* to regain kids' attention. When they respond by raising their hands and focusing on you, have pairs take turns reporting the results of their discussions. Then have one person in each pair read **Philippians 4:8-9** and the other summarize it in one sentence. Ask:

◆ **How could following the instructions of Philippians 4:8-9 help you live each day in a good-attitude zone?** (By helping us focus on the good things in life; by keeping us from thinking too long about things that bring us down; by reminding us to think about Jesus because he's good and worthy of praise.)

◆ **Why do you think the Bible tells us to think about good, positive things?** (So we'll keep a good attitude; because God is good; because it'll help us enjoy life.)

◆ **What gets in the way of your following the advice of Philippians 4:8-9 each day?** (I get distracted by problems; I get mad when things don't go my way; I forget to check my attitude.)

◆ **What can you do this week to improve your attitude zone and fulfill the instructions of Philippians 4:8-9?** (Read my Bible; pray; hang out with positive people; encourage others.)

Say: **We don't have to get trapped in a bad-attitude zone because** 📖 **God's people can be positive and joyful regardless of the circumstance.**

THE POINT 📖

LEARNING LAB

THE UNLIKELY HERO 📖

(8 to 13 minutes)

Say: **Bad attitudes can be catching. But even when everyone around us has a negative attitude, we can remain positive and joyful. Let's listen to a story about a person who refused to give in to negative attitudes.**

Play "The Unlikely Hero" from the *cassette*. Afterward form groups of no more than three and direct students to number off within their groups.

Say: **Discuss the next few questions in your group. Then I'll call out a number from one to three. The person in your group whose number I call out will be responsible for sharing your answer. Here's my first question:**

◆ **What was the best part of this story for you?** (When Theodore won; when Theodore convinced everyone else that he could do it.)

◆ **When have you felt like Theodore?** (When I really believed I could do something, but no one else did; when my friends refused to help me do something special.)

◆ **How did Theodore's positive attitude help him overcome the negative expectations of the others?** (It helped him keep going even when the others refused to help him; it gave him courage.)

◆ **Why do you think people rallied around Theodore in the end?** (Because he changed their attitudes; because they were encouraged by his example.)

Have each group member read one of the following portions of the story of David and Goliath in **1 Samuel 17:22-24, 32-37,** and **40-50.**

◆ **How are Theodore and David alike?** (Neither of them gave up; they both succeeded in spite what others thought.)

◆ **How could David maintain such a positive attitude when everyone else thought Goliath would kill him?** (He trusted in God for courage; he knew God was in control.)

◆ **How do people sometimes take the steam out of your positive attitudes?** (They make fun of me; they want me to gripe with them; they tell me I'll never succeed.)

◆ **What can we learn about maintaining a positive attitude from the examples of Theodore and David?** (We don't have to go along with the crowd's negative attitudes; we can trust in God no matter what obstacles we face.)

Say: **Sometimes it's easy to give in to the negative attitudes that surround us and spend our time on griping, complaining, or simply giving up. Next time you're tempted to do that, remember Theodore and David and that ✍ God's people can be positive and joyful regardless of the circumstance.**

✏ **THE POINT**

TABLE™
TENT

We believe Christian education extends beyond the classroom into the home. Photocopy the "Table Tent" handout (p. 160) for this week and send it home with your kids. Encourage kids and parents to use the handout to spark meaningful discussion on this week's topic. Follow up next week by asking kids how their discussions went with their families.

CLOSING

WARM FUZZIES

(2 to 7 minutes)

LEARNING LAB

If you skipped the previous activity, form trios. Have trio members take turns answering this question:

◆ **What's one important thing you've learned today?** (God's people can be positive and joyful; my attitude affects how much I enjoy life; I can maintain a positive attitude even when others don't.)

While kids are answering the question, cut the *fuzzy fleece* into pieces to make enough "warm fuzzies" for everyone to have two. (If you're able to cut the *fuzzy fleece* into pieces before class, you'll save time during class.) Be sure to cut extras in case you need them.

Say: **We've learned a lot today about how ✍ God's people can be positive and joyful regardless of the circumstance. Now let's take a minute to recognize the positive**

✏ **THE POINT**

and joyful attitudes right here.

Give each person two of the warm fuzzies you made from the *fuzzy fleece*.

Say: **Think about your trio partners and a way each one has contributed a positive and joyful attitude to our class today. For example, you might say, "Josh has really been enthusiastic about doing all the activities" or "Christy has been so cheerful all through class."**

Once you've got your ideas, give your partners each a warm fuzzy and tell them how you've noticed their positive and joyful attitudes today.

Give kids a few minutes to complete this activity before moving on to the "Quarter Review."

LEARNING LAB

QUARTER REVIEW

REFLECTION

(3 to 8 minutes)

Form a circle and pass the Learning Lab with all the Learning Lab items in it around the circle. Have everyone choose one item out of the box that reminds them of something they've learned over the past quarter.

Next, have kids take turns telling why they chose the items they did and what experiences from the past 13 lessons their items remind them of. Then have kids take turns completing these sentences:

◆ This Learning Lab item helped me learn...

◆ One Scripture from the past class sessions that's encouraged me is...

◆ One thing I'll do differently because of something I learned in this class is...

Dismiss with a prayer of thanks for all your kids have learned through this course.

Convince Me

Photocopy and cut apart the four sets of instructions below for the "Convince Me" activity. You'll need one set of instructions for each person in class.

Your task is to persuade your leader to balance the *plastic bat* on the palm of his or her hand for two seconds. Whine, beg, and plead to convince your leader. Say things like "Pleeease," "You never do what I want you to do," and "Do it for me."

C'mon! Do it for me! Pleeease! C'mon! Do it for me! Pleeease! You never do what I want.

Your task is to persuade your leader to balance the *plastic bat* on the palm of his or her hand for two seconds. Use peer pressure to convince your leader. Say things like "Everyone does it," "Cool people always balance bats on their palms," and "It'll make you more popular."

Everyone does it. It'll make you more popular. It's cool. Everyone does it. It'll make you more popular. It's cool.

Your task is to persuade your leader to balance the *plastic bat* on the palm of his or her hand for two seconds. Use logic to convince your leader. Say things like "You've done a lot of things; you can balance a tiny bat on your palm," "It's simple! A baby could do it," and "You'll never do it if you don't try."

A baby could do it. It's simple. You'll never do it if you don't try. It's simple. You've done lot of things.

Your task is to persuade your leader to balance the *plastic bat* on the palm of his or her hand for two seconds. Use threats to convince your leader. Say things like "I won't like you or be your friend if you don't balance the bat," "You'll make me angry if you don't balance the bat. You don't want to see me angry, do you?" and "Do it or I'll cry."

Do it or I'll cry. You'll make me angry. You don't want to see me angry. Do it or I'll cry. You'll make me angry.

TABLE™ TENT

TABLE™ TENT

"I thank my God for every time I remember you, always praying with joy for all of you" (Philippians 1:3).

Talk Triggers

▲ How would you describe a positive and joyful attitude?

▲ Why can Christians be positive and joyful in their daily lives?

THE WORD on Be-Awesome Attitudes

Monday   Acts 16:22-34
What situations make you feel like a prisoner? How can you imitate Paul and Silas' joyful attitudes in those situations?

Tuesday   2 Corinthians 2:14a
How can you maintain a positive attitude when "victory" seems far away?

Wednesday   2 Corinthians 4:16-18
Describe a time when hope for God's future helped you keep a positive attitude.

Thursday   James 1:2-4
How can you find joy in today's troubles?

Friday   Isaiah 40:31
How can God help your attitude to "rise up as an eagle in the sky" this weekend?

Saturday   Romans 8:35-39
How does the promise of Romans 8:35-39 affect your outlook on life? Explain.

BONUS IDEAS

GREAT GAMES

Learning Lab Olympics—Set up the following events and have kids compete individually or in small groups in a "Learning Lab Olympics." Award prizes to kids who score the most points.

◆ *Birdie in the Hat*—Place the *mini straw hat* face up on the floor. Have kids line up 10 feet away from the hat and "fly" the *twirlybird* into the hat. Kids get 500 points if any part of the *twirlybird* touches the hat and 1,000 points if the *twirlybird* lands inside the upturned hat.

◆ *Flipper Fun*—Give each person a *flipper* and have kids line up their *flippers* on the edge of a table. Have kids simultaneously flip their *flippers* toward the opposite edge. See who can make his or her *flipper* land closest to the edge without falling off the table. Award 1,000 points for first place, 750 points for second, and 500 points for third.

◆ *On the Spot*—Tie the *elastic strips* together. Have kids take turns standing on the *fuzzy fleece* and jumping rope with the *elastic strips*. Kids must land with at least one foot on the *fuzzy fleece* after every jump. Award 1,000 points to the person who successfully jumps the longest, 750 to the second longest jumper, and 500 points to the third longest jumper. For added difficulty, require both feet to land on the *fuzzy fleece* after each jump.

◆ *"Holy Books" Lip Sync*—Have kids perform lip-sync concerts of "The Holy Books" from the *cassette*. Award 2,000 points for each of the following categories: most original, most professional, most humorous, and best costumes.

The Vine and the Branches—Select one volunteer to be the "vine" and have that person wear the *carpenter wreath* on his or her ankle. Have everyone else line up on one side of the room. On "go," have the vine tag as many other students as

possible, without allowing the wreath to fall off his or her ankle.

When a student has been tagged, he or she must become a "branch" by locking elbows with the vine or other branches. Once attached, branches must help the vine tag other students. The game is over when everyone is attached to the vine.

After the game, use **John 15:1-11** as the basis for a discussion about how Jesus is the Eternal Vine, and we are his branches.

Backward Baseball—Use the *squeeze ball* and *plastic bat* for a game of Backward Baseball. Tell kids the rules are the same as regular baseball but with the following exceptions:
◆ batters must hold the bat with both hands behind their backs,
◆ everyone (including base runners) must run backward during the game (caution kids to look behind themselves as they run),
◆ only the pitcher can use his or her dominant hand when throwing the ball, and
◆ no strikeouts allowed.

After the game, lead kids in a discussion about how Christians can approach life from a different perspective. Use **Romans 12:1-2** as the basis for your discussion. Now, play ball!

Blow Ball—Lay the *checked mat* on the floor and place the *squeeze ball* in the middle. Form two teams—team A and team B. Have team members spread out around the *checked mat*.

Turn on "Blow Ball" from the *cassette* to start the game. Tell team A to blow the *squeeze ball* so that it ends up on a black square when the music stops; tell team B to blow so that the *squeeze ball* ends up on a white square when the music stops. Randomly stop the tape and award points to the team whose square the ball is on at that time.

AFFIRMATION ACTIVITIES ▬▬

Personalized Passages—Have each student write a personalized Bible verse on a 3×5 card as encouragement for a partner. To personalize a verse, ask kids to write out their chosen passages, substituting their partners' names where appropriate. Here are a few examples of how your kids can personalize a passage:

◆ **John 3:16** ("God loved you, Nate, so much that he gave his one and only Son so that if you believe in him you may not be lost, but have eternal life.")

◆ **John 14:3** ("Jesus said, 'After I go and prepare a place for you, Erin, I will come back and take you to be with me so that you may be where I am.' ")

◆ **Romans 8:10b** ("The Spirit gives you life, Andy, because Christ made you right with God.")

◆ **Matthew 28:20** ("Jesus said, 'I will be with Christy always, even until the end of this age.' ")

◆ **2 Corinthians 5:17** ("Because you belong to Christ, David, you are a new creation.")

Tell kids to read their personalized passages the next time they need encouragement to face life's struggles.

It's in the Mail—Give each person a 6×9-inch Manila envelope and colored markers. Have kids decorate and write their names on their envelopes. When everyone is done, tape the envelopes in a row on the wall.

Say: **These envelopes will be our "encouragement mailboxes" for the next month. Each time you come to class, we'll take a minute or two to write encouraging notes to each other and place them in our mailboxes. Then we'll check our mailboxes at the end of class each week.**

Pass out paper and pencils, then have kids write the first of their encouraging notes. Kids might write notes telling why they admire other class members, how much they appreciate a person's friendship, what they've learned about God from each other, special Bible verses, or anything else positive and uplifting.

Fresh-Scented Experiences—Form a circle and give each person one of the *scented stones*. Have kids take turns describing in one word or phrase the aroma of the stones. For example, kids might say, "like springtime," "fresh," or "clean."

Next read aloud **Colossians 3:12-14.** Ask:

◆ **How would following the instructions of Colossians 3:12-14 bring a fresh, pleasant "aroma" to our lives and the lives of others?**

◆ **What attitude changes would you need to make to follow the instructions of Colossians 3:12-14 this week?**

Retrieve the *scented stones*. Take one stone and give it to the person on your left as you complete this sentence: "One way you bring a fresh, pleasant attitude to this class is..."

You might finish the sentence by saying, "in the way you

encourage others" or "in the way you smile so easily." Next have that student repeat the process for the person on his or her left. Continue until the stone has been passed around the entire circle.

PARTIES AND PROJECTS

Bible-Character Parade—Plan a parade around the theme of overcoming life's obstacles. Map out a route through church grounds or your community, then have kids walk the route on the designated day. Some ideas for the event:

◆ Kids could dress up as favorite Bible characters who overcame obstacles in life. Kids might dress up as Noah, King David, Ruth, Esther, or any of the apostles.

◆ Kids could brainstorm and create a float on the back of a truck that demonstrates the theme. Have parents donate old newspapers, chicken wire, and paint for the float. Kids might make a float depicting Noah and the great flood. Or they could create a boxing ring where a character labeled "Life's Obstacles" is down for the count.

◆ Kids could dress up as clowns and pass out cards and balloons that have encouraging Scripture verses printed on them.

Have the parade route end at an open area on the church grounds or at a park. Have plenty of refreshments there for kids and their families to enjoy after the parade.

Cemetery Session—Help your kids experience the hope of eternal life in Christ with a Saturday morning visit to a local cemetery.

Gather kids in a grassy area inside the cemetery and ask:

◆ **What do cemeteries make you think of? Explain.**

◆ **How could a cemetery be a place of hope for Christians?**

Form pairs and give paper and pencils to each pair. Send kids out to look for tombstone inscriptions that reflect the hope of eternal life in Christ. Have kids copy the inscriptions on their papers. For example, kids might write, "Safe in his Savior's arms" or "To live is Christ, to die is gain." Tell kids they have 15 minutes to complete their explorations.

When everyone returns, have kids share their discoveries. Then have pairs read **1 Corinthians 15:50-58.** Ask:

TEACHER TIP

Although it's not always required, it's usually best to ask permission from the organization that oversees the cemetery before taking your kids there. You might also want to ask for parents' permission before allowing a student to join your cemetery trip.

◆ **What do these tombstone inscriptions and Scripture verses mean to you?**

◆ **If you were to write a tombstone inscription that reflects your own hope of eternal life with Christ, what would it say?**

Lead kids in a prayer of thanks for God's gift of eternal life. Then go out for brunch to celebrate!

"You" Party—Have students plan and throw a party where the emphasis is on "you" and not "me." Try these activities:

◆ ***"I" Ban***—Give each person 10 toothpicks. Every time a student says the word "I," someone may take a toothpick from him or her. Give a prize to the person who ends up with the most toothpicks at the end of the party.

◆ ***Getting to Know You***—Play this icebreaker that requires students to learn more about each other. Make a list of 10 general characteristics of people in your class. For example, your list might include "someone who likes rap music" or "someone who has a bird for a pet." Give everyone a copy of the list and a pencil.

Tell kids to find someone who fits a characteristic you've listed and have that person initial the appropriate item. No one can initial more than two items on a list. Give kids three minutes to complete the activity. Award a prize to the person with the most initialed items when time is up.

◆ ***The Search for "U"***—Hold a scavenger hunt for things that begin with the letter "u," such as an umbrella, an ugly tie, or a map of the USA. Serve "u"-shaped cookies and upside-down cake.

Teacher Notes

Teacher Notes